New Beginnings in Ministry

Edited by James H. Murphy

New Beginnings
in Ministry

THE COLUMBA PRESS

1992

First edition, 1992, published by
THE COLUMBA PRESS
93 The Rise, Mount Merrion, Blackrock, Co Dublin, Ireland

Cover by Bill Bolger
Origination by The Columba Press
Printed in Ireland by Colour Books, Dublin

ISBN: 1 85607 057 3

Contents

Foreword

But there are also many other things which Jesus did;
were every one of them written,
I suppose that the world itself
could not contain the books that would be written.
Jn 21:25

St John's gospel ends by covering itself quite deftly against the charge that it has not said all that there is to say about the life of Jesus. The subject of Christian ministry, too, is such a vast one that no single book could deal with all its facets. Certainly, this book of essays from a Catholic perspective does not attempt to do so. Its authors have chosen to focus on three areas of particular concern to them.

The *Sitz im Leben* of all ministry is the Christian community. In the section, *Ministry and Christian Experience*, Thomas Curran reflects eloquently on his own experience of ministry in Peru. Eamonn Conway offers a theological analysis of the experience of God, or lack of it, in a contemporary Ireland fast assimilating the consumerist patterns of living so common in other western societies. Tess Harper argues for a connectedness with the authentic rhythms of life as a means of recovering a sense of the spiritual. And Patrick Collins sets out his vision of the necessary components for faith in today's world.

At the heart of these essays is the section, *New Beginnings in Ministry*, from which the entire volume derives its title. Its authors are advocates of a challenging agenda. By means of parable as well as argument, Robert Whiteside maintains that a focus on tasks is damaging to ministry and that the most effective minister is the 'playful contemplative.' After reflecting on her own experience of an institution in change, Moya Curran argues that the only way in which Church personnel will be able to cope with accelerating change is through fostering an inner calm. A creative response to the crisis in traditional ministry in the Church would entail empowering and financing lay people, especially women, the young and retired people, she concludes. Finally, Thomas McHugh reviews the British experience of twenty years of the Rite of Christian Initiation of Adults. For him it is 'a way of being Church' which is 'beginning to challenge the Church's addiction to the male, celibate, clerically-controlled model of Church and ministry.'

The flowering of collaborative ministry has raised many questions concerning the priesthood. In the section, *A Future for the Ordained Ministry*, three scholars attempt to tackle some of these questions. Thomas Lane uses the word prosopon/persona as a prism for bringing the relationship between the ministry of the ordained and non-ordained into focus. Brian M. Nolan sets the role of the priest in the context of a view of the Church as 'a communion of communions.' In doing so he touches on questions concerning the Petrine ministry, the rite of ordination, the celibacy of the clergy and the ordination of women.Eugene Duffy discusses the formation of candidates for priesthood in the light of history and of a recent papal document. He suggests that the local Church rather than a seminary might be the more appropriate *locus* for the formation of the priests of tomorrow.

Anyone familiar with the authors of this book will know that, almost without exception, they are associated with All Hallows College in Dublin, the missionary seminary which has trained over four thousand Irish priests for service in dioceses abroad. In 1992 it celebrates the one hundred and fiftieth anniversary of its foundation. John Joe Spring's concluding essay pays an affectionate and yet perceptive tribute to the sense of mission which continues to inspire it.

New Beginnings in Ministry is dedicated to the graduates of All Hallows, to all those who have answered the call over those one hundred and fifty years to 'Go, teach all nations.'

PART I

Ministry and Christian Experience

A Ministry in Latin America

Thomas Curran

Ministry is always conditioned by the situation in which it is exercised. We minister to a particular people, at a particular time and in a particular place; and all these factors affect how we exercise our ministry.

Ministry in Peru, at this particular time in its history, is ministering to a people who are afflicted by ever-deepening poverty, by violence, both institutional and subversive, by illness and disease which have become endemic because of the poverty in which they flourish, and yet, withall, to a people of deep and sincere faith in a God who loves them.

'Rarely in Peru has been seen such suffering and death, such darkness and despair; yet, at the same time, such solidarity and creative capacity, so many seeds of life which must not be lost.' So started a recent letter signed by over a thousand priests and pastoral agents. Since it was written the crisis has deepened. The death-toll has risen steadily as the Shining Path guerrillas continue their ruthless and blood-thirsty campaign for power. Priests, religious, police, military, public figures and simple peasants, all alike have fallen to their merciless sickle. The killing in February of a young mother who had dared organise the other poor mothers of her neighbourhood to confront them was the most notable, but by no means the only one of its kind. The utter cold-bloodedness of her killing has aroused, as nothing else has done, the revulsion of poor people. She was shot in the presence of her children at a community fundraising event which she had helped to organise in her poor 'barrio', and her body dynamited as she lay dying. The threat is constant and we all minister under it. The lack of a social conscience on the part of the government as it pursues neo-liberal policies, which

---

they hope will ensure Peru's reinsertion in the world's financial community, means that the poor get poorer as consumer taxes are levied on everything they eat, wear or use. This in a country where the basic minimum wage was recently raised from $38 to $72 a month, and where that $72 barely covers 20% of the needs of a family for a month. A great part of our ministry to the poor has to be just helping them to stay alive. Against that background all our ministry takes place.

To help coordinate the various works of a parish here, I find it useful to think of the Church as being the continuing presence of Christ in the community - Christ in his threefold ministry as prophet, priest and king. The prophetic ministry of the parish is exercised in the various works of evangelisation, the priestly ministry in participative celebration of the eucharist and the other sacraments, and the kingly ministry in the various works of administration and social service (Christ, the king who serves his people).

Evangelisation is a dynamic ministry here. There would be no Church if it weren't for the generosity of thousands of lay-people, many of them young, who offer their services as catechists every year. They prepare for this ministry over a period of four years with annual month-long summer schools and occasional retreats. I have about a hundred people involved in this ministry in my parish of 60,000. Gradually the emphasis in our catechetical programmes is moving towards family catechesis in which the parents are encouraged to take more responsibility for preparing their children for the reception of the sacraments. We are only in our second year of this programme and already the results seem quite dramatic. It has had a marked effect in drawing back to the Church couples who had distanced themselves from it.

The preparation for the sacraments of baptism and marriage is also in the hands of lay-people. As pastor, my efforts mainly go into the training of the teams of laity who so willingly take on these ministries.

There are other groups in training as future leaders of basic ecclesial communities. They are following a programme which is designed to deepen their knowledge of Christ in his humanity so that they can better appreciate his divinity. It is heart-warming to be part of their discussions, for they really know their Lord.

The liturgical ministry has proved to be a rich opportunity for involving lay-people as lectors, eucharistic ministers and leaders of paraliturgies. They gather weekly, about twenty of them, to reflect on the readings for the following Sunday and prepare brief introductions to each, and also prayers of the faithful arising out of their present reality. They, by their very enthusiasm, give the answer to the problem that plagues all our efforts at evangelisation: How to be 'good news' in a death-dealing situation? The Lord is a palpable presence for these people. He accompanies them on their hard and hazardous journey, and they never seem to question his love for them. They really are the people of God.

Celebration comes easy to Peruvians. They celebrate birthdays, weddings, baptisms and patronal feasts. So our worship ministry is ploughing in fertile fields.

The flower of this ministry is the team of women who visit the sick, bringing them communion weekly. They have recruited the sick as participants in the apostolate of the parish. And it is humbling to see people of deep faith willingly enter into the apostolate of redemptive suffering, uniting their sufferings with those of Christ. I have never been so conscious of walking in the presence of saints, and the monthly Mass for the sick on the first Friday is a joy and a delight.

The presence of Christ as servant-king is expressed in our administration and social service ministries. With such outright poverty, hunger, malnutrition and disease, this is a very active ministry. There are twenty soup-kitchens in the parish – organised by the people themselves and supported by the Church and other welfare organisations. By pooling their meagre resources, they feed about four thousand people one meal a day. A team of parish volunteers keeps in touch with all the soup-kitchens on a weekly basis, and so we manage to keep aware of the most urgent cases of need. Another group runs a parish pharmacy where we try to help people with basic medicines at less than half of the market price. An outgrowth of the various social service ministries is the conscientisation of people who themselves are perhaps not so cruelly touched by the often appalling conditions. This, in time, generally leads to the growth of a human rights commission.

A parish library provides access to basic text-books in use in schools and colleges, and reference works for students in higher education. The library owes its existence to the generosity of a family in Omaha who provided the seed grant to get it going, and to the dedication of a dozen young people who took the ball and ran with it. The library is now the proud owner of a computer, thanks to the generosity of a pastor in Miami. This may help give an edge for the first time to students from this area who are studying computer technology.

Two weeks ago a young optometrist offered his services to the parish – eye examinations for a nominal fee. I can hardly get in the door of the parish centre for the crowds of poor, young and old, who are turning up. A lawyer comes once a week to provide free legal advice to the poor – a very valuable service in a country where law is a veritable jungle. A young psychologist comes for three hours every evening to help with the myriad problems that arise in this fertile breeding ground.

When I reflect on my ministry here, certain insights emerge. Before coming I had to come to terms with the fact that, after all my efforts, Peru would probably be poorer and worse off than it was before I came. Despite that fact, it would still be worth doing. And so it has proved. My ministry has become very much one of 'affirming the brethren', as Jesus enjoined on Peter. There is a wealth of willing talent, of people, young and old, who are only too anxious to respond to any challenge that is placed before them. I have a sense of 'calling forth' talents that are lying dormant just waiting for the word to bring them to life.

This leads on to my next insight (if that is what it is): that God is a God of life. In the midst of conditions that deal death and degradation, this is a very important value. The struggle for survival takes up much of the energy of many of my people. To see them come from that to ecclesial community meetings that deal with topics touching on new life in the kingdom, here and now, is exhilarating. Sometimes we missionaries say that we seem to feel more keenly than they do the hurt and the injustice that are their daily lot.

Another insight that I value is that we ask God for miracles and he gives us seeds. The trick is to see the miracle of life that is contained in every seed, the miracle of future growth. My prejudices and preferences often blind me to that, of course. I try to overcome that by consulting as widely as I can on projects and suggestions.

The best way of nurturing the kind of growth the parish needs is by giving responsibility to people for the various ministries and their offshoots. It took over a year of building trusting relationships for that to begin to happen. But happen it did.

Central to all our efforts is a consciousness of being the hands and feet of Christ. Peruvian Catholics have a deep awareness of his presence and his interest. There is probably a tendency to be more conscious of the crucified than the risen Christ. But they easily and lovingly grow into the idea of carrying on his saving work. I have had memorable discussions with them on the gospel passage of the disciples on the road to Emmaus.

We know that Christ is most effectively incarnated at the point of greatest need. In a city of such need we don't have to look far to find him. Christ's method of dealing with human need was to empty himself, taking on the form of a servant, so that he might enter into the human condition in all its poverty. That method has not changed. For us that means, above all, accompanying our people, very often feeling their helplessness, but trying to remain faithful in that ministry in spite of all. And, somehow or other, growth comes.

An underlying principle in all our efforts is that of forming disciples in the model of Christ. There is a four-year, once a week course at archdiocesan level for the training of pastoral agents. There is a variety of summer schools, from Gustavo Gutierrez's course in liberation theology to the various catechetical courses. Gospel discussions, prayer and retreats are a great help towards that end. It is essential to see the Church as a community for forming disciples rather than as an organisation for getting things done. Things get done, of course. Indeed the growth is often chaotic. But the essential thing is that disciples have been formed a little bit more in the process.

The role of the priest is that of custodian of the vision, a vision which is formed and clarified in prayer, scripture study and community reflection. Reflection on the reality in which the people live is an essential part of the process of forming this vision. The conditions may not seem to lend themselves to vision, but without it there is no pastoral leadership. The document I quoted earlier ends: 'Let us not renounce the vision, the project, the utopia of a country of justice, freedom, liberty, participation and solidarity. Let all of us construct it from the poor and the marginalised, and build it in our life today, which is part of the tomorrow we seek.'

I would like to underline that the involvement of laity is not something that stems from the fact of my being the only priest in such a large parish. It is their baptismal right and duty. Clericalism and the reservation of ministries to clergy alone I see as an obstacle to the spread of the gospel. Where the Church is vital and dynamic in Latin America is where the laity have accepted the responsibilities that accrue to their baptism, and have been allowed and encouraged to do so.

Finally, let me say that I would not sleep at night if I thought of all that I am not doing. All I know is that what I am doing means that I need that sleep. And so, conscience-stricken or not, I sleep.

'The Price of Sparrows'
Experiencing God Today

Eamonn Conway

Introduction
Religion is in decline in Ireland. Many questions spring to mind.
Why are fewer people experiencing active and involved membership of the Church as fulfilling? Why does the prevailing attitude of
the media to the Church fluctuate between hostility and indiffer-
ence? Why are fundamentalist movements within and without the
Church increasing in popularity? Why are some people no longer
searching for God, while others seem to believe quite readily in
apparitions, healings and other apparent manifestations of the
supernatural? Why is there an alarming decline in the number of
candidates for ordained ministry?

The Second Vatican Council's Constitution on Divine Revelation
reminds us that 'it pleased God, in his goodness and wisdom, to reveal himself and to make known the mystery of his will.'1 Yet fewer
people seem to experience God's self-revelation in any meaningful
way today. This is why religion is in decline. In this paper I intend
to examine how adequately we interpret our experience of God today. This will involve both a study of theological method and of the
mission of Jesus Christ and the Church. I presuppose here that experience of God is possible, that is, that God exists and is present to
us.2

'Experience of God' – what is meant?
A shared understanding of what we mean by 'experience of God'
cannot be presumed. *Experience* results from the encounter between
the individual and reality. Experiences are lodged in a memory
bank which we partially inherit from and partially share with society. We relate new experiences to previous ones. In this way, for
example, previous knowledge is confirmed and illusions are shat-

tered. New experiences, in turn, join in forming the horizon for future experiences.

It is only when we sift through our experiences for meaning that the question of experiencing God arises. When we search for ulti-mate meaning we are searching for a motif which unifies our life, which grounds it, gives it direction and purpose. The search for happiness, wholeness, love, certainty, hope and success is a quest for such meaning. Experiences of alienation, isolation and disinteg-ration, as well as of achievement, acceptance and forgiveness, cause us to reflect on 'how it is' ultimately with reality as a whole. As Walter Kasper says, 'When man ceases to ask about the whole, he will have evolved back into a clever animal.' [3]

Enquiry about the meaning of reality as a whole is already enquiry about God. God is not one object, among others, 'out there in reali-ty'. God is the ground, the goal and the horizon of all that is.[4] This is why God is not experienced directly. God is co-experienced in smiles and tears, in anxiety and fear, as well as in calm and joy.

Interpreting experience today
Because God is co-experienced, changes in the way we experience the world, in how we relate to ourselves, each other and our envi-ronment, affect our recognition of encounters with God. Today it is more difficult to forge a unifying motif for human experience through which we become conscious of God's presence. In fact, it is easier today to avoid the pain sometimes involved in such a weld-ing process. I wish to highlight here just two ways in which the interpretation of human experience can be curtailed or reduced to-day.

The first is that our rapidly expanding consumerist society, a society of 'instant everything,' can laminate us from what is deepest within us. We can move rapidly at the flick of a mental button from one 'high' to another whenever our boredom threshold is reached, without even realising we are doing so, until something happens to make us stop in our tracks in disturbing puzzlement. Perhaps for many today the only occurrences of this kind are serious illness and death. Such occurrences still awaken us to the fragility of our understanding and send us scurrying off in search of ultimate meaning.[5]

The second is a suspicion of authority which effects how we interpret our experience. A community should provide the horizon of understanding (wisdom) within which our individual human experiences can be understood, a horizon which each of us gradually appropriates and to which each of us, in turn, contributes. We should refer our own interpretation of our experiences to the wider wisdom of the community to see if it is valid. Today, however, we are forced to choose between the conflicting claims to authority and wisdom of various agencies (media, Church, politicians, advertisers).[6] For many, personal experience is now self-authenticating. There is a danger of an arbitrary subjectivism or emotivism in this shift 'from the experience of authority to the authority of personal experience.'[7]

It cannot be denied that there were real dangers in the contrary over-reliance on an external and alienating authority. Loyalty to authority, for example, was valued over authenticity, relevance and meaning. However, when there is an over-reliance on personal experience which is not referred for verification to the wider experience of the community, genuine meaning and relevance can be displaced by merely emotivist expressions of preference. When emotivism takes over, as M.P. Gallagher points out, 'I feel like it' and 'I don't feel like it' become common yardsticks for serious decisions.[8]

Interpreting experience of God today
Both the difficulty of finding time for reflection in a rapidly-moving society and the danger of subjectivism reduce or curtail valid interpretation of our experiences. They also spawn a reductionist understanding of God. An inadequate, 'vulgar' theism can prove a greater block to authentic interpretation of encounters with God than no understanding of God at all. [9]

Today believers are less likely to be troubled by rationalists asking them to show how belief in God is reasonable. The crisis today is not one of facts but of relevance. Today people want to know how belief in God will make life meaningful. This is difficult to explain if meaning has been reduced to an arbitrary subjectivism; if what is 'meaningful' is 'what makes me feel good' at any particular time.

In addition, there is a danger of reacting, rather than of responding, to the openness to God we encounter today among those who still hunger for meaning and relevance. Arguably, fundamentalism both within and without the Roman Catholic Church is such a reaction. Fundamentalism panders primarily to people's emotions. Drawing on a naïve and uncritical interpretation of scripture, it feeds an inadequate notion of God, a God very often created in people's own image and likeness. For a time this eases hunger pains which are important signals of deeper privation. But it fails ultimately to nourish, leaving people in a famished state especially when confronted with the incomprehensibility of suffering and evil.

Finally, and perhaps more importantly, there is always a risk of a reduction when we discuss God in the context of the meaning of human existence, however thoroughly meaning is pursued. A relationship with God gives human life value and purpose, indeed the most profound value and purpose. But in our anxiety to give our lives meaning and purpose there is always a danger of assigning God *merely* a role or a function. There is a risk that God becomes of interest only to the extent that God is of use to us. Such a consumerist attitude to God reduces both God's dignity and ours.

Mediating God as God – a challenge for the theologian
In an effort to avoid a consumerist attitude to God, it would be natural to turn to the theologian for guidance. Theology's task, after all, is to mediate an *understanding* of Christian faith, hope and love. However, since René Descartes (1596-1650) acknowledged the collapse of medieval cosmology and looked inward for an unshakeable foundation for knowledge, theology has had particular difficulty mediating Christian faith meaningfully and faithfully at the same time. The problem has been to develop a theological method which is anthropologically sensitive, yet which leaves God intact.

One of the problems Descartes encountered in his search for certitude was the possibility that he could be deceived into thinking that he existed when in fact he did not. If God is good and true, argues Descartes, surely God will prevent this from happening? For Descartes, then, knowledge of God occurs in the medium of human subjectivity and God's role is primarily functional. John O'Donnell claims that something 'pernicious' happens at this point: God's existence becomes dependent upon human subjectivity and God is now wholly at the disposal of human self-fulfilment.[10] A logical outcome is the recognition that God must be disposed of, if human self-fulfilment is to be realised. This is precisely the atheistic philosophy of Ludwig Feuerbach for whom 'God' is merely a cipher for the human being's own infinity and absoluteness.

Theology attempted to take the 'anthropological turn' seriously. Immanuel Kant (1724-1804) set out to provide a firm rational basis for knowledge of God but seemed to succeed in destroying all possibility of so doing. Karl Rahner (1904-1984), familiar with the work both of Maurice Blondel and Joseph Maréchal, and influenced by Martin Heidegger, made the best attempt in recent times at overcoming the Kantian problem.

Rahner's main thesis is that anthropology is essentially deficient christology. A careful examination of the structures of human being and knowing demonstrates that the human spirit is, from the very outset, beckoned beyond the self toward union with God and others. Such a study makes us aware that we dwell 'at the edge of the infinite ocean of mystery' which we do not always see because we are forever occupied with the grains of sand along the shore.[11] At the very edge of human experience we find ourselves listening for a possible revelation of a hitherto unknown God. Should God not have revealed himself, argues Rahner, then the greatest human perfection would have been to stand waiting and listening before God's silence.[12] Yet God chooses to reveal God's self through a plan of revelation which has a dynamism towards incarnation from the very beginning. In Christian dogma, therefore, we find the highest expression of human potential. In this way Christology fulfils anthropology.[13]

Rahner takes anthropology seriously, yet avoids asserting the reality of God on the basis of the human spirit's openness and desire for God, which is the mistake of German idealism.[14] Is Rahner then well placed to mediate Christian faith faithfully and meaningfully at the same time? Rahner recognises how many people are alienated and estranged from Christian faith and he shows that divine revelation corresponds to the deepest hopes and desires of humanity. But there are two difficulties.

The first is that, due to the way in which interpretation of human experience today becomes so easily truncated, many people are not only alienated from Christian faith but also from their own deepest hopes and desires. If people no longer search for, or expect, a unifying motif for their experiences, even a theological method as anthropologically sensitive as Rahner's is unable to penetrate and mediate faith meaningfully and credibly.[15] In fact, if people interpret human experience in such a way that the God-question does not arise, all theology is severely crippled. [16]

The second difficulty relates to the danger mentioned earlier of a consumerist attitude to God. Rahner's method presents divine revelation as corresponding to the deepest hopes and aspirations of humankind, and only that. This is Hans Urs von Balthasar's main gripe with the anthropological approach to theology:

> It might be true that from the very beginning man was created to be disposed toward God's revelation, so that with God's grace even the sinner can accept all revelation. *Gratia supponit naturam.* But when God sends his own living Word to his creatures, he does so, not to instruct them about the mysteries of the world, nor primarily to fulfil their deepest needs and yearnings. Rather he communicates and actively demonstrates such unheard-of things that man feels not satisfied but awestruck by a love which he never could have hoped to experience. For who would have dared describe God as love, without having first received the revelation of the Trinity in the acceptance of the cross by the Son?[17]

Rowan Williams points out that Rahner's Christ is the answer to the human question, whereas Balthasar's Christ 'remains a question to all human answers.'[18] Surely we look to the theologian to mediate to us fully both aspects of the one mystery of Christ because, through Jesus of Nazareth, humanity's deepest needs and yearnings are fulfilled by a love, the depth of which puzzles us, which we could never have adequately anticipated, and still only inadequately appreciate. In the wake of this love we are both heartened and challenged.

Letting God be God – as Christ did

Jesus Christ is the sacrament of God's love. The Church, as the sacrament of Christ, is to re-present and effect the mystery of God's love in the world. In a unique way, then, the Church is entrusted with enabling people to experience God. Ways the Church could do this more effectively might emerge from a study of Jesus' experience of God and its effects. We begin with the effects.

Jesus was convinced of the ultimate worth of human life. This conviction was the source of his power.[19] Because of Jesus' faith in the power of goodness and truth, he did not need and did not accept any other authority. As Nolan puts it, Jesus did not make authority his truth; truth was his only authority.[20] In this way it was impossible for authority, as Jesus exercised it, to be experienced by people as alienating or as imposed upon their experiences from outside. The parables, for example, frequently began or ended with questions which challenged the listener to recognise that what Jesus was saying was the self-evident truth about reality: 'What is your opinion? A man had two sons ...' (Mt 21:28); 'Which of these three, do you think, proved himself a neighbour to the man who fell into the brigands' hands?' (Lk 10:36); 'Which will love him more?' (Lk 7:42)

In addition, Jesus' faith gave him what we might refer to today as a robust self-image that liberated him from control and manipulation by others. Jesus was a free man.[21] He was free to keep company with those who most needed him, with those whose vision of the ultimate meaningfulness of human life had been blurred, with those whose sense of their own worth and dignity had long since

been eroded. He bodied forth God's particular and extravagant
love:

> 'Are not five sparrows sold for two pennies? And not one of
> them is forgotten before God. Why, even the hairs of your head
> are all numbered. Fear not; you are of more value than many
> sparrows.'[22]

Jesus' power and freedom sprang from his experience of God. He
experienced God in such a way that he was convinced that God
meant nothing but goodness and love for humanity. Jesus allowed
God to express goodness and love in and through him in a unique
way. He accepted God as God, and this gave him a tremendous
serenity and, at the same time, an urgent sense of mission.[23] Jesus
acted upon his conviction about God and he committed his life to
awakening a similar conviction in others. He remained faithful to
his conviction to the point of death.[24] Jesus' resurrection testifies
that even death has no power to destroy such faith. [25]

Experiencing God today – the mission of the Church
Jesus' experience of God, and his witnessing to this experience by
his actions, are normative for the Christian community. We speak
frequently of the importance of witness. The Christian community
will only succeed in its mission when Christians testify to their experience of God by the way they live their lives. But witness is not
an imposition on Christians. Genuine witness inevitably emanates,
freely and joyfully, from a correctly interpreted experience of God.
Why does bearing witness often seem such a burden today?

At this point we can begin to look a little more closely at the Irish
context. Despite the Church's enormous investment in education
here there has been, nonetheless, a failure to 'hand on the faith'. To
some extent we have succeeded in communicating that aspect of
Christian faith which consists of a system of values or mores,
summed up in John 13 as 'Love one another ...' We have been less
successful in creating or sustaining a kerygmatic Christian community in which the second part of this commandment, '... as I have
loved you,' is experienced. It is only in the context of such an experience that the entire love-commandment seems reasonable and vi-

able. This helps us to understand why people in Ireland appear to be 'picking at the package' and why we talk of *à la carte* Catholicism today. Ireland has failed to 'hand on the faith' because what Kavanagh once said of Lough Derg can be said of our island as a whole: the twentieth century blows across it now. Consumerism and subjectivism will make experience of God as difficult in Ireland as elsewhere. How can we respond?

The questions of experience of God and of human dignity are inseparable. An impoverishment or enrichment in our understanding of our experience of God is matched by a loss or gain in terms of our dignity. Restoration of human dignity is at the heart of the gospel and therefore forms the core of the Church's mission in every age.[26] The Church is effective in its mission only when the forces in society which blind, deafen and cripple people are overcome.

Jesus understood himself as sent especially to those whose dignity was compromised by both religious and civil institutions of the time. As the New Testament relates, each person who met Jesus, and whose disposition was ultimately, however vaguely expressed or understood, one of faith and not of despair, had a renewed sense of dignity and self-worth. Sometimes this inner healing was expressed in a physical way, but this was secondary. Of more importance was the experience of being at one with God, others, and oneself.

To be able to restore dignity to others we must ourselves be convinced of the ultimate value of human life, and of our own dignity. In a society such as ours, which is becoming increasingly materialistic, the Christian community has a responsibility to ensure that a person's value is understood as intrinsic, and not as something measured according to criteria of usefulness determined by a minority who control market forces.

In this context, one problem in Ireland which demands the urgent attention of the Christian community is unemployment. Through work we contribute to our own development and the development of society. Without working it is difficult to hold on to a sense of dignity and self-respect.[27] There are three steps Christians could take to enhance dignity and self-worth and bring about the kind of society in which God's presence is more easily felt.

First, while there is a shortage of jobs in Ireland, there is not, strictly speaking, a shortage of work. There are many ways in which people can and do contribute creatively and valuably to the fabric of Irish society. In fact, we have an extraordinarily high number of people who care for the young and the old, support married couples, console the bereaved, and provide and maintain facilities which make all of this possible. Much of this work is done 'voluntarily', sometimes on a full-time basis by people who are considered 'unemployed'. Because these people survive financially on social welfare assistance, they carry the stigma of being 'unemployed', of being dependent, of 'getting something for nothing.' This stigma is unfair and unjust. There is no shortage of work in Ireland, only paid jobs. A re-think is called for.

The second relates to the existing paid jobs in Ireland and is more radical. Work-sharing, with an inevitable decline in the quality of life in terms of possessions and conveniences for some, would give everyone the opportunity of a more balanced life-style, with time and energy for 'being' as well as 'doing', and a greater opportunity to reflect and wonder. [28]

Third, the Church itself can provide employment opportunities for people who are already trained in pastoral ministry and frustrated at the dearth of opportunities to put their expertise at the disposal of the Christian community. Failure to do this affects the sincerity of the Church's preaching on employment as well as the realisation of its mission.

Conclusion
If we feel that we do not encounter God today, or cannot recognise God at the root of our everyday experience, we have to accept that somehow we, by the way we live our lives, have 'plugged ourselves out'. God still loves the world.

It might seem foolish to attempt to reconstruct society along Christian lines. It would be, if it were not for the fact that through Jesus of Nazareth we experience God's love for us, and in Jesus of Nazareth we encounter one human being who was transformed by God's love. God gave Jesus the power and the freedom to transform society. Market forces did not dictate the extent of Jesus' love. The power of love to change should not be underestimated.

The Second Vatican Council reminds Christians that they share in the prophetic mission of Christ.[29] Prophets are, as Rahner puts it, none other than believers who can express their own experience of God correctly.[30] Prophets put their own experience of God at the disposal of others in such a way that they (others) can see faith in God as the purest and most profound expression of their own experience of life. It was precisely in this sense that Jesus was prophetic.

If we could fully experience God's love for us, if we could see ourselves even for one moment as God sees us, as salt of the earth and light of the world (Mt 5:13-14), we would be transformed people. We would realise our dignity and our self-respect, for God's acceptance of us brings self-acceptance and acceptance of others. We would give up constructing plastic paradises. We would be liberated of our possessiveness. We would have more, simply by desiring less. We would be free.

Notes

1   Dei Verbum, n 2 (reference to Eph 1:9).

2   Atheism and sceptical positivism (which restricts the human search for meaning, claiming that the only data accessible to the human being comes in and through the natural sciences) are therefore rejected as fundamentally false.

3   Möglichkeiten der Gotteserfahrung heute, Geist und Leben 42, 1969, p 333.

4   The following quotations, one from a mystic, the other from a theologian, help clarify the Christian notion of God:

"'Excuse me,' said one ocean fish to another, "you are older and more experienced than I, and will probably be able to help

me. Tell me: where can I find this thing they call the Ocean?
I've been searching for it everywhere to no avail." "The ocean,"
said the older fish, "is what you are swimming in now." "Oh
this? But this is only water. What I'm searching for is the
Ocean," said the young fish, feeling quite disappointed as he
swam away to search elsewhere.' (A. de Mello, *Song of the Bird*,
India, Diaz del Rio, 1982, p 14).

'That God really does not exist who operates and functions as
an individual being alongside of other beings, and who would
thus, as it were, be a member of the larger household of all reality. Anyone in search of such a God is searching for a false God.
Both atheism and a more vulgar form of theism labour under
the same false notion of God, only the former denies it while
the latter believes it can make sense of it. Both are basically
false: the latter, the notion that vulgar theism has, because this
God does not exist; and the former, atheism, because God is the
most radical, the most original, and in a certain sense the most
self-evident reality.' (K. Rahner, *Grundkurs des Glaubens.
Einführung in den Begriff des Christentums*, Freiburg, Herder,
1976, p 72).

5   As K. Rahner writes: 'This, then, is the situation in which we
find ourselves: we are all sitting in the prison of our own existence as in a condemned man's cell, waiting until our turn
comes. Until then one can play cards, enjoy a condemned
man's last meal, and forget for the moment that the prison door
will soon open and we will be called out for our final journey.
But that is precisely what we must not forget. The animal is
blind to its approaching death, or has at most some dim fear of
losing its life. But we are aware of death and must not suppress
this awareness. We should live with death in our view. We
know that we shall simply be thrust into the unyielding loneliness of death where no one can accompany us any further,
where the chatter stops. The only thing that still counts is what
one can take with one in death: that is I myself as I was in the
ultimate depths of my own heart, that heart that was full of
love or full of spite and selfishness, a nuisance to myself and

others. We take nothing with us into this state of abandonment
except what we ourselves are in the ultimate and radical decision of our own hearts. Already in the here and now we must
weigh our life day by day on the scales of death with a view to
being able one day to die our own death. We should practise,
even in this life, how to die ...' (*Was heist Auferstehung? Medita-
tionen zu Karfreitag und Ostern*, Freiburg, Herder, 1985, pp 9-10).

6   This is not the only cause of the contemporary suspicion of authority, which has its roots in the Enlightenment. The Enlightenment led to disillusionment with all claims to authority
which were not empirically verifiable, including that of Christianity. Characteristic of the Post-Enlightenment period is disillusionment with being disillusioned. Recognising how unhar-
nessed technologically-based progress has destroyed much of
the environment and how the human imagination has been so
devastatingly circumscribed, even science's claim to authority
is suspect.

7   The post-synodal apostolic exhortation, *Pastores Dabo Vobis*
(John Paul II, March, 1992), concerning priestly formation,
comments (n 7): 'We should take note also of a desperate
defence of personal *subjectivity* which tends to close it off in in-
dividualism, rendering it incapable of true human relationships. As a result, many, especially children and young people,
seek to compensate for this loneliness with substitutes of various kinds, in more or less acute forms of hedonism or flight
from responsibility. Prisoners of the fleeting moment, they
seek to 'consume' the strongest and most gratifying individual
experiences at the level of immediate emotions and sensations,
inevitably finding themselves indifferent and 'paralysed', as it
were, when they come face to face with the summons to embark upon a life project which includes a spiritual and religious
dimension and a commitment to solidarity.' Cf. A. McIntyre,
After virtue. A study in moral theory, London, Duckworth, 1981,
p 222ff; D. Lane, *The experience of God*, Dublin, Veritas, 1981, p
10ff; M.P. Gallagher, *Struggles of Faith*, Dublin, Columba Press,
1990, p 51ff.

8   M.P. Gallagher, *Struggles of Faith*, p 51.

9   Cf Note 4 above.

10   J. O'Donnell, *The mystery of the triune God*, London, Sheed and Ward, 1988, p 7-11. Cf. W. Kasper, *The God of Jesus Christ*, London, SCM, 1984, p 18ff; E. Jungel, *God as the mystery of the world*, Edinburgh, T.&T. Clark, 1983, p 111ff.

11   K. Rahner, The experience of God, *Theological Investigations 11*, London, DLT, 1974, p 159.

12   This is the thesis of Rahner's second major work, *Horer des Wortes*, which appeared in 1940.

13   Rahner proposes an interlocking (*Verschränkung*) between philosophy and theology. Only in this way can he 'give people confidence in Christian dogma such that they can believe with intellectual honesty.' (*Grundkurs des Glaubens*, 33).

14   Rahner avoids the reductionist position of German idealism because for him there is no such thing as a purely philosophical system. As J. Ratzinger notes, '(Rahner's) transcendental method does not pretend to deduce Christianity purely from itself (i.e. this method); it is a presupposition of understanding which becomes possible because faith had already opened up the field of thought.' (Vom Verstehen des Glaubens. Anmerkungen zu Rahners *Grundkurs des Glaubens*, *Theologische Revue* 74, 1978, p 184). Cf K. Lehmann, 'Karl Rahner. Ein Portrat' in K. Lehmann and A Raffelt, *Rechenschafts des Glaubens*, Karl Rahner-Lesebuch, Freiburg, Herder, 1979, p 33.

15   Rowan Williams comments on Rahner's theological method: 'We must in some degree know our own hearts before we can recognise the heart's desire which is the Incarnate God.' ('Balthasar and Rahner' in J. Riches, Ed, *The analogy of beauty*, Edinburgh, T. & T. Clark, 1986, p 18.

16   As W. Kasper notes, 'It is possibly one of the most severe challenges to believers (at least to those who have to preach the faith) that there is an increasing number of people who lead a

happy and fulfilled life without any belief in God. They seem to lack nothing that faith could give them ... faith is like money that is no longer backed up by the hard currency of human experience. This worrying dichotomy between faith and human experience is so pervasive that faith threatens to become a mere superstructure. Therefore, one of theology's most urgent concerns must be to restore the 'location' (*Sitz im Leben*) to faith and to apply itself to the theme of faith and experience (*An introduction to Christian faith*, London, Burns and Oates, 1980, pp 19-20.

17 H. U. von Balthasar,'Current trends in Catholic theology and the responsibility of the Christian,' *Communio*, Spring 1978, p 80.

18 'Balthasar and Rahner' in J. Riches, Ed, *The analogy of beauty*, p 34. In his anxiety to protect the unpredictability and wonder of the historical Christ-event, Balthasar, in his own theological method, plays down the human capacity to anticipate divine revelation. As Claude Geffre says, '... von Balthasar himself cannot do wholly without some kind of pre-understanding. I can only apprehend the beauty of the mystery of Christ if I already have within me some kind of norm of beauty, and it is because I perceive there a certain affinity that I can come to credibility.' ('Recent developments in fundamental theology: an interpretation,' *Concilium* 5, 1969, p 11).

19 'The power of faith is the power of goodness and truth which is the power of God.' (A. Nolan, *Jesus before Christianity*, London, DLT, 1977, p 84.

20 *Jesus before Christianity*, p 123.

21 We are told that Jesus was not 'afraid of anyone' and that 'a man's rank' meant nothing to him.(Mk 12:14) He was neither controlled by his family (Mk 3:21) nor by the religious leaders of the time.(Mk 3:22) He was unconcerned about his reputation.(Mt 11:16-19, 7:39; Jn 4:27, 9:24) Jesus was a free man because nearness to God amplifies rather than diminishes human freedom.

22 Lk 12:6-7.

23 Cf Lk 11:2, 10-12, 12:22-26.

24 Cf Lk 22:41-43.

25 Cf Heb 12:2; Gal 2:20 and 3:23.

26 Cf Is 61:1-2, Luke 4:18.

27 'Through work man must earn his daily bread and contribute
    to the continual advance of science and technology and, above
    all, to elevating unceasingly the cultural and moral level of
    society within which he lives ... Work is one of the characteris-
    tics that distinguish man from the rest of the creatures ... work
    bears a particular mark of man and humanity.'(*Laborem Exer-
    cens*, Introduction).

28 The Mayo theologian, Donal Dorr, outlines such a proposal. Cf.
    'Exile and return' in E. McDonagh, Ed, *Faith and the Hungry
    Grass*, Dublin, Columba Press, 1990, pp 75-77.

29 *Lumen Gentium*, n 31.

30 *Grundkurs des Glaubens*, 163.

Learning from a Celtic World
Masculine/Feminine Balance

Tess Harper

In speaking about masculine/feminine balance it is perhaps a safe starting point to say that we experience in western modern society an imbalance, and that this is why the topic needs to be addressed. I find the tools that psychologist C.G. Jung devised are very helpful in clarifying what is involved in masculine/feminine balance in the first place.

I would like to outline some of these tools with the hope that they can offer a different way of looking at gender balance. Then I will look at the Celtic world from an intuitive rather than solely historical point of view and will reflect on my own lifestyle which involves trying to live in right relationship.

Jung uses the terms animus and anima to describe the counter-sexual element in the psyche. Therefore a woman has within her an inner man, so to speak, and this is her animus character. A man likewise has an inner woman, his anima.

The anima figure is built up from the man's childhood experience of his mother. If his relationship with his mother was primarily positive then his anima figure will be primarily positive. If he hated his mother, then he will hate the woman within him. A man's relationship with his mother will determine how he relates to other women in his life. Part of a man's life journey involves separating himself from his mother, and from the mother within, and developing a free relationship with women in his life, and with the woman within himself.

Jung also talks of projection. By this he means that the unconscious material in the psyche is automatically projected outwards, onto people or things. This is a natural process and is one of the ways that the unconscious material is accessible to us. Once a projection happens, ideally we can name it and then attempt to withdraw it from the other person or object. This all sounds very simple! However, in reality it is not. Most of the time we are not aware that we are projecting the contents of our own inner world onto others. For example, if I really detest something in another's behaviour, nine times out of ten, if I am honest, I can find a similar trait in myself of which I was not aware. Rather than take responsibility for this and attempt to change or accept my own behaviour, it is easier to dislike the other person and either avoid them or attack them!

A man who has not yet begun to relate to the woman within himself, will project her onto other women. So, how he relates to women is how he relates to his own inner woman.

The anima for a man is the realm of his feelings, his intuitions, emotions, wisdom, his experience of connectedness to others and to the world around him. This is if his relationship to her is positive. If he ignores her, abuses her, or represses her (i.e. if he does these things to his own feelings) then she manifests herself negatively. She attacks him by sucking him into dark moods, he feels depressed, is irritable and experiences a sense of meaninglessness.

The animus for a woman is her inner man. He also will be projected onto men if he is not recognised and claimed. If a woman is in a positive relationship with her animus figure (both the anima and animus appear in a person's dream with many different faces and attributes, they are in fact not a singular character) he will be her torch-bearer. He will enable her to focus, to create, to articulate and to relate to the outer world. If her relationship with him is negative he will come across in dogmatic statements. The woman will sound arrogant, opinionated and pushy. A woman possessed by her animus will come across as a pseudo-man. A woman with an under-developed animus will appear to be diffused and unfocused, in a world of her own.

If a person can relate to their counter-sexual element they can experience life in a balanced way. A woman can be creative, assertive and articulate without losing her essential feminine nature. A man can be artistic, feeling and sensitive, without being swallowed by the anima and becoming moody or without repressing and hating women in an attempt to control his own inner women.

All of this, I feel, is useful in understanding masculine/feminine balance in our society and the lack of it. In our modern, technological, consumer, western society men seem to have inherited the habit of repressing the feminine – both in themselves and the women around them. They are expected to control their feelings, and likewise they control women in the same way. Patriarchal society, as we experience it today, has within it chronic inequalities towards women. In an attempt to address these very serious injustices, women are now competing in a male world for equal rights in that male world. This is a justice issue. It is only fair that women are paid the same as men for the same work done and that they get equal opportunities.

I do not wish to denigrate the very powerful and brave work done by many women who have spent their lives bringing these injustices to the public eye. The issue of masculine/feminine balance, however, within ourselves and between the genders, is not addressed in this justice issue. The justice issue does not look at the dominant attitudes of society and address how these dominant priorities are themselves unhealthy. Attitudes, for example, such as production, consumerism and competition, disconnect us from the natural world, from our natural rhythms, from ourselves/others and from a relationship with the divine. In achieving equal rights in a masculine-oriented technologically-based milieu, and in competing in this masculine dominated world for equal rights, women are in danger of losing their connection with their own essential feminine nature. This is a nature which is connected to natural rhythms.

The structure of modern society disconnects us from our true feminine and also true masculine selves. It is dominated by a masculine mind-set. When women get equal opportunity within this world they are expected to perform in the same way as men perform. It is pretending to be a genderless world where men and women can all do the same kind of work. And yet it is not genderless, it is masculine! For example, in the business world women are expected to be focused, to be efficient, to be rational. Women can, of course, be all of these things. Yet during a woman's menstruation, in the workplace, she is not really to be taken seriously because she is perhaps a little more irritable – it is 'that time of the month'. There is also the awkward intrusion of her wanting to have a child and interrupting her work with maternity leave. Pre-menstrual tension is at an all-time high nowadays and I wonder is there a connection between this and the fact that, to be efficient and productive and successful in the modern work force, you must become disconnected from you body, which for a woman means that you become disconnected from what is essentially feminine? Men too must suffer from this disconnection from their bodies.

In addressing the masculine/feminine imbalance in modern western society, if one is willing to look further than the economic and social imbalance, one begins to see just how modern western society disconnects us from our own bodies, from the land, from our food, from each other, and from the true source of our gender.

If one wishes to speak in terms of mission and ministry, it is my belief that there is a great need to live a life that attempts to be re-connected to the tradition of our country, to the rhythms of the land, to the rhythms of our own bodies and gender, to re-establish right relationship with the world around us.

Modern western society has lost right relationship in so many ways. For example, with regard to the food we eat. The way we treat animals demonstrates this: with factory farming, battery hens, hormone-pumped cattle, tethered sows who never move beyond the four by three feet of cement space that they are constantly chained to until they will be slaughtered. We are very familiar with buying out-of-season vegetables, plastic-wrapped, that have travelled across the world and have been sprayed with God knows what to keep them from going limp! Small organic farmers have had their produce refused in shops in the past because ordinary, normal vegetables from the ground down the road did not look as well as the shiny abnormally big produce that can be imported.

We have lost right relationship with each other. The extended family has largely collapsed, in the cities especially. The nuclear family now exists where people go out to work, often travelling many miles by car, then come home in the evening to watch television. Of course, none of this is necessarily wrong. However, I suspect it does not answer our deeper needs for connection, for feeling part of a larger community, for relationship with the rhythms of nature, and for a deeper understanding of what it is to be woman and what it is to be man.

The word Celtic has come to symbolise much more than the historic race of Celts. The Celts were the inheritors of a non-patriarchial society in Ireland. This meant that women enjoyed freedom and rights that were denied to the contemporary Roman women. For example, a woman could become head of the family, could rule, could be a prophetess, an educator. She could also inherit part of her mother's or father's property. Apart from this, however, I believe the word Celtic has become a symbol in people's minds. For me personally it is a term that gathers in the much older tradition of Ireland, the old myths of the Tuatha de Danann, the pre-Celtic peoples, and somehow for me it speaks of a way of being in the world which has deep respect for nature, for the other, and for the Divine.

I feel the term Celtic can be used to describe something which we can strive for – for balance and right relationship and respect. The Irish people have a strong culture and have a strong sense of family, of where they come from, and of relationship with place. I have found, living in a house that welcomes people to visit and to partake of our lifestyle, that many people are keenly aware of the longing in their bodies and souls for a less frenzied way of living. Often the word Celtic captures what it is they are longing for. The early Irish church had a spirituality that was not caught up on dogmas or sexuality. The monks worked the land and lived at the heart of the clan. It is said that when they went to work in the fields, they would bring the Blessed Sacrament with them and hang it from a branch of a tree in the field they were in. God was all around, in their work, in their prayer. The island of Inis Mór off the coast of Galway, where I live, is rich in spirituality. There are early prehistoric forts, which some believe the early peoples used for worship, and many monastic sites. The very land has a sense of holiness about it that many visitors notice and call different names. Ireland is filled with similar sites – holy wells, standing stones, stone crosses. Our spirituality is in our Gaelic language where the most common greeting is 'Dia dhuit', 'God be with you.' The early Irish monks lived with a sense of the 'Holy' in the ordinary.

I live with a group of people who try to live self-sufficiently, and who keep animals to be in relationship with them. We also grow our own food, and offer hospitality to people who wish to share our lifesyle. Often we have had young city people visit. One young person exclaimed when asked to pick some vegetables from the garden, 'I'm not eating that. It came out of the dirty soil!' The milk from the goat created some unpleasantness also when they realised it came from the animal's 'dirty' tit! How far removed from living in some relation ship to the food you eat? It is not essential that you grow it yourself, but it is important to know where it came from and what methods were used in farming it. And in the case of animals, we should ask whether these animals receive any respect whatsoever, did they get any kind of a fair life, or were they merely products to be organised, crowded in, fattened up, and slaughtered?

In nearly seven years of living a lifestyle that attempts at self-sufficiency, hospitality, simplicity, with a strong Irish tradition and spiritual base, we have learnt more than all the colleges and courses in the world could offer!

At first we would go down to the gardens to plant seeds with a book on how to do it under our arms! Over the years we have often been late in laying sea-weed for fertiliser, in planting potatoes, in cleaning the gardens. But the journey from the head to the body eventually showed results and now we know in our bodies. We find we are tuned into the rhythms of the seasons and of the sowing more and more. Certainly we still find ourselves well behind islanders who have done this kind of thing all their lives! Yet we are more aware of the right time for doing things than when we first started. From a training that sat me behind a desk for most of the day and pumped my head with facts, I have learned to shepherd sheep and goats, keep fowl and sow potatoes. I have also learned how to work a Macintosh computer and how to co-edit a magazine, Aisling, that acts as a forum for the ideas we try to live by.

Modern western society has moved far away from right relationship. Our very lives are in danger with what is called 'the environmental crises.' Our souls are in danger of being sucked into the fantasy that more possessions mean happiness and security. Our rich experience of ourselves as woman/man is being threatened by the 'genderless genre' enthusiasm. Our experience of ourselves in Ireland as people with a rich and empowering heritage is being pushed aside for a Coca-Cola, MacDonalds mono-culture.

Thankfully more and more people are asking the question, 'What can I do?' I firmly believe each and every person can do something. They can look deep within themselves to their deepest desires and dreams and then seriously ask why they are not living them out. This, perhaps, is the primary relationship to get right – the relationship with the self within. From there a person can look at all the relationships in their lives and see if they are healthy, if they are respect-filled and loving. These include relationship with the earth we walk on, with the food we eat, with the people we live with, and with the people we affect by our actions (for example, who are we affecting when we buy multinational products which were produced by the equivalent of slave labour in Two-Thirds World countries?).

The imbalance between the genders in our western society is one example of where modern western society fails in right relationship. There are many more. I find in our Celtic heritage a rich resource for trying to re-establish right relationship – with the earth, with animals, with ourselves, with one another as men and women, and with God.

Faith and Ministry

Patrick Collins

A number of years ago I heard a parable which made quite an impression on me. In its naïve way it described what could be referred to as life's crucifixion points of powerlessness. They are the moments of vulnerability when we consciously encounter our desperate need for God. As such they are the birthplaces of faith.

A blackbird and a crow lived in the same tree. The blackbird used to sing sweetly and effortlessly from dawn to dusk. As for the crow, no matter how hard he tried, he could only squawk. He thought to himself, 'If I observe the blackbird closely, I may discover the secret of her singing.' After a while he did notice that she had a different diet from his. He changed his, but to no avail. He continued to squawk. Then he noted that the blackbird had a different timetable from his. So he trained himself to imitate her pattern of waking and sleeping. It made no difference however. He still continued to squawk. When he told a couple of passing jackdaws about his problem, they informed him about a school for birds some miles away. 'Why not go there for a year or two,' they said, 'and take a course in music? When you qualify, you may be able to sing like a blackbird.' The crow heeded their advice. For two arduous years he learned about the theory and practice of music. When he returned to his tree, the blackbird was still there singing as sweetly as ever. The crow flew to the highest branch, took in a deep breath, proudly opened his beak, and launched into a squawk! The moral of the story? No matter how hard he tries, a crow will never be able to sing like a blackbird.

It seems to me that the same is true in our lives. In spite of our intelligence, knowledge, experience, skills, efforts and good intentions, there are many things we cannot change. As contingent creatures, for example, we will never be the adequate explanation of our own existence. As sinners we can neither earn nor merit the saving grace of God. Nor can we live out our lives in accordance with the Lord's will. Speaking on behalf of of us all, St Paul said, 'I do not do the good I want. But the evil I do not want is what I do ... Wretched person that I am, who will save me from this body of death?'(Rom 7:19,24) Like the hapless crow in the parable, we have to come to terms with such crucifixion points of powerlessness. Time and time again, in the midst of our mission and ministry, we have to acknowledge that all will be lost if God does not sustain us. That is where faith comes in. It is the quality or power which enables the things we desire in our powerlessness to finally become, by the grace of God, the things we experience.

Faith in contemporary thought
Like a many-sided diamond, the subject of faith has been examined in recent years from various overlapping points of view. In a well known description, Paul Tillich[1] has referred to religious faith as the state of being ultimately concerned with what is truly and solely ultimate, namely, the ineffable mystery of God. Martin Buber[2], a Jewish writer, has explored the distinction between interpersonal and propositional notions of faith. Cantwell Smith[3] has furthered this approach by meticulously examining the evolving relationship between interpersonal faith and different forms of belief, from an historical point of view. In recent years, rather than focusing on the content of faith, James Fowler[4] has focused on faith as a universal activity. It can mature through six developmental stages, each of which is characterised by increasing degrees of cognitive complexity and comprehensiveness, which may or may not have a religious content.

Bernard Lonergan[5] who described faith as 'knowledge born of love,' maintains that such a disposition has to be incarnated anew in our culture which is in a process of fundamental change. It is moving from 'classical' to 'historical' forms of consciousness, i.e. from a static world view, which stresses the importance of objective authority, to a dynamic one, which stresses the importance of sub-

jective experience. The current crisis of faith, he says, is a misno-
mer. In fact it is essentially a cultural crisis which requires a refor-
mulation of 'the faith' in contemporary categories of thought. Otherwise it will appear to be increasingly irrelevant in a fast changing
world. Lonergan's observation reminds me of a story about an im-
migrant boy in New York city. When asked if his family had found
a home yet, he answered, 'We have a home already, we just have to
find a house to put it in.' A final point. Avery Dulles[6] has suggested
that currently there are three models of faith operating in people's
lives, the *intellectualist approach*, of a person like St Thomas Aquinas, i.e. faith as doctrine; the *fiducial approach*, of a person like St
Therese of Lisieux, i.e. faith as trust; and the *performative approach*,
of a person like St Vincent de Paul, i.e. faith as commitment and
action.

While being aware of the importance of these interrelated points of
view, I will not be focusing on them here. Rather, I will reflect, with
the help of scripture, on three kinds of faith of the saving, trusting
and charismatic kind. They have become increasingly important to
me in recent years. I am including the third form for three main reasons. Firstly, it seems to me that when Jesus referred to faith, he often had the charismatic kind in mind. Secondly, the faith to do
deeds of power, such as healings and miracles, is neglected in modern theology, exegesis and spirituality. Thirdly, I believe that this
sort of faith has an important role to play in present day evangelisation and ministry.

Saving Faith

What is known as the theological virtue of justifying faith is the
bedrock of the Christian life. As Jesus said before his ascension,
'Whoever believes and is baptised will be saved.'(Mk 16:16) Like
the apostles before him, Paul had discovered that, 'Faith comes by
hearing the message ... and how can people hear without someone
preaching to them?'(Rom 10:17;14) For example, when the jailer in
a Philippian prison suspected that all his prisoners had escaped following an earthquake, he decided to commit suicide. As soon he realised this St Paul shouted, 'Don't harm yourself! We are all here.'
Having brought them out, we are told that the jailer 'rushed and

fell trembling before Paul and Silas.' Evidently, he had reached a decisive crucifixion point of powerlessness. Acutely aware of his urgent need, he at last found words to express what he had probably felt in a vague, inarticulate way, many times in the past. 'Men, what must I do to be saved?' he cried out on his own behalf and on behalf countless numbers of people down the ages.

Paul responded to this all-important question, by giving a one line summary of the gospel. 'Believe in the Lord Jesus,' he said, 'and you will be saved - you and your household.' (Acts 16:25-35) This reply echoed what he had written on other occasions: 'If you confess with your mouth, "Jesus is Lord," and believe in your heart that God raised him from the dead, you will be saved.' And again: 'Everyone who calls on the name of the Lord will be saved.'(Rom 10:10;13) Presumably Paul went on to expand on his succinct answer, by telling the the jailer about the core truths of Christianity, which are sometimes referred to as the *kerygma*,[7] e.g. 1 Cor 15:3-8. Like the jailer and his household, the Acts repeatedly attest that those who greeted the good news with faith were baptised immediately. By receiving the sacrament of initiation they were immersed, drenched, soaked and innundated in the saving grace of Christ the Lord.

The Foundations of Faith
Nowadays most people are baptised as infants. But it seems to me that many of us have failed to appropriate consciously the saving grace of the sacraments through personal faith in the foundational truths of the Christian faith, i.e. the *kerygma*. In fact, as I have suggested elsewhere,[8] we are currently living through what could be called a kerygmatic crisis of head, heart and hands.

The kerygmatic crisis of the *head* refers to *knowledge*, i.e. to do with intellectualist faith. Many Christians today are ignorant of the basic teachings of the scriptures, and their primary importance within the hierarchy of revealed truth. As a result, they fail to appreciate the fact that, for example, the divinity of Christ is of greater significance than the assumption of Mary or any moral teaching.

The kerygmatic crisis of the *heart* refers to *awareness*, i.e. to do with fiducial faith. Even when they have a notional grasp of the good news, many Christians fail to experience the liberating power of God's unrestricted mercy and love in their personal lives.

The kerygmatic crisis of the *hands* refers to *action*, i.e. to do with performative faith. Is it any surprise that those who neither know nor experience the power of the *kerygma* in their lives, fail to witness to it in their words or actions? All too often they seem to live like those who have not been baptised. They appear to separate religion from life and to walk by sight and not by faith. St James posed a relevant question in this regard when he asked, 'What good is it, my brothers and sisters, if you say you have faith but do not have works? ... faith by itself, if it has no works, is dead.'(Jas 2:14;17)

Because the Catholic Church sometimes wrongly presumes that all its members are evangelised, it places the full yoke of discipleship on their shoulders, e.g. with regard to sexual and marital morality. If such people have not come into a personal relationship with Christ or experienced his extraordinary mercy and love, they may have the *desire* to carry the yoke the Church places on them, but they will not have the *power* to do so. For example, a baptised couple will find that even if they neither attend mass or pray, they won't have much difficulty being married in Church. As man and wife however, they will be prevented from using contraceptives, or getting an abortion. If in time the marriage fails, they will find that it is impossible to get a divorce and almost impossible to get an annulment or to be married again in church.

Without being evangelised, the Christian ethic is not a 'yoke that is easy and a burden that is light.'(cf Mt 11:30) Instead of being a way of liberation it can become a way of oppression. Perhaps Jesus would say to the Church authorities of our day, 'Woe to you teachers of the law and Pharisees, you hypocrites! ... you tie up heavy loads and put them on people's shoulders, but are not willing to lift a finger to move them.'(Mt 23:23;4) Is it any wonder that many baptised Christians turn their back on the Church because they associate it with bad rather than good news? What is needed is evangelisation, a kerygmatic proclamation which is aimed at head, heart and hands, by people who have already experienced its liberating power in their own personal lives.

Catholic and Protestant views of salvation

In the light of the last point, I suppose it is not surprising to find that committed evangelical Protestants sincerely believe that, in spite of being baptised, many if not most Catholics are not saved. In their view, RCs are not born again because they fail to make a conscious decision to give their lives to Jesus Christ, by accepting him as their personal Lord and Saviour. Billy Graham, the renowned Protestant evangelist, makes this typical appeal to his listeners and readers alike: 'If you have never accepted Christ into your life, I invite you to do it right now before another minute passes. Simply tell God you know you are a sinner, and you are sorry for your sins. Tell him you believe Jesus Christ died for you, and that you want to give your life to him right now, to follow him as Lord the rest of your life. "For God so loved the world, that he gave his only begotten Son, that whoever believes in him should not perish, but have eternal life."(Jn 3:16).'9 Graham then goes on to assure the born again that all their sins are forgiven and that they are new creations in Christ. Over the years I have been moved, edified and inspired by Protestant men and women who have testified to this type of salvation experience. That said, I have come to see that, in spite of its obvious merits, this challenging point of view can have a number of limitations.

Firstly, in my experience many evangelicals are inclined to talk about salvation in the past tense, as something they have already experienced in a definitive way. But surely it is something ongoing?(cf 1 Cor 1:18) While it may have already begun, salvation will only come to fruition if the person *being saved* continues to cooperate with the grace of God. Secondly, some 'saved' Christians can have a problem admitting serious sins they may have committed after their salvation experience. This is so because they seem to be so incompatible with the grace they claim to have received. This can lead either to a certain blindness where wrong-doing is concerned, or in some cases to a morbid sense of defeat and despair. Thirdly, those who believe that they are already saved sometimes suffer from an off-putting self-righteousness. They believe that a majority of mankind, including many of their fellow Christians, are on the path to perdition, no matter how good and sincere they might seem to be. Fourthly, those who stress the evangelical understanding of salvation are often quite poor at building upon that foundation stone. Instead of developing an elaborated spirituality which takes account of the purgative, illuminative and unitive stages of spiritual growth, they are inclined to keep going back to the milk of the foundational experience.(cf Heb 5:12) Fifthly, I have noticed that some evangelical Christians seem to overlook the material needs of the poor and to be surprisingly uncritical of the socio-political status quo. Jim Wallis, a Protestant himself, has written a brilliant and relevant critique of the political complacency of many evangelical Christians.[10] Lastly, because they seem to overlook the fact that their theological outlook is conditioned by things like historical circumstances and a rather literalist reading of Scripture, they fail to appreciate the Catholic experience of salvation.

While the Protestant approach might not make much sense to a majority of Catholics, the goodness, love and fidelity of many RCs provide ample evidence of the fact that they are indeed experiencing saving grace. By participating in a sacramental community this precious gift can be appropriated by means of an on-going process of osmosis and conversion. Having begun in baptism,[11] it often occurs in a real, but largely non-conceptual way, e.g. by making a good general confession during a parish mission, attending Mass with devotion, etc. This explains why, although many devout Catholics fail to express their experience of redemption in a formula of words which would satisfy the expectations of evangelical Protestants, their *experience* is essentially the same as that of 'born-again' Christians. However, they do succeed in avoiding some of the limitations characteristic of a fundamentalist interpretation of salvation. That said, I'm convinced that we believing Catholics and Protestants have a lot to learn from each other and our respective faith experiences of saving grace. We can evaluate our differing approaches by using Jesus' rule of discernment when he observed, 'By their fruit you will recognise them'(Mt 7:16), and again, 'Not everyone who says to me, "Lord, Lord," will enter the kingdom of heaven, but only the one who does the will of my Father in heaven,'(Mt 7:21), e.g. being willing to be merciful as God is merciful.(cf Lk 6:36). As someone has observed, we are no closer to God than we are to our enemy.

In the light of points like these, surely Catholics and Protestants alike need to ask themselves the following three questions, either in biblical terms like these or in a more contemporary way that takes cognisance of our secular ways of thinking: What is the good news of salvation? Secondly, is it good news for you personally? Thirdly, how would you express that good news in concise, relevant down-to-earth language? For my own part, I would attempt to answer the questions in the following way.

We are all sinners who have been influenced by the spirit of evil. But Jesus has shown us, particularly by his death on the cross, that there is no need to be afraid of God's justice or his punishments. Though very real, they are on hold, so to speak, until the day of judgement. Meantime we live in the age of God's unrestricted and unconditional mercy and love. If we look only into the eyes of his mercy, expecting only mercy, we will receive only mercy, now and at the hour of our death. Afterwards we will rise to see the Lord, not as in a glass darkly, but face to face forever.

Over the years, this good news message has filtered down from my head to my heart. As it has done so, it has progressively banished the unholy fear of God that I used to experience. Instead it has provided me with the power in Paul's words, 'to grasp how wide and long and high and deep is the love of Christ, and to know this love that surpasses knowledge.'(Eph 3:18-19) In the light of that inner awareness of love, I know what St John meant when he wrote, 'There is no fear in love, for perfect love casts out fear; for fear has to do punishment.'(1 Jn 4:18) On a number of occasions this realisation has flooded me with interior consolation and brought tears of joy to my eyes. In prayer I try to renew and deepen this sense of salvation in Christ so that I might express it in my daily life. I realise that the extent to which I fail to be merciful as God is merciful (cf Lk

6:36-39) in my dealings with others, is the extent to which I will lose the inward ability of accepting that I am accepted by the Lord.

Salvation, Mission and Ministry

This on-going sense of being saved by being united to Christ and blessed by the Spirit is vital and indispensable in Christian life, mission and ministry, for, 'unless the Lord build the house, in vain do the labourers build.'(Ps 127:1) Knowledge, qualifications, elbow grease and sincerity are no substitute for this awareness. As St Vincent de Paul said to one of his missioners, 'The work you are about to undertake is not just the work of man; it is the work of God. *Grande Opus*. It is the continuation of what Jesus Christ was given to do, and consequently human effort will end up spoiling everything if God is not involved in everything we try to do. Neither philosophy nor theology nor preaching is effective where people's souls are concerned. It is necessary that Jesus Christ associate himself with us; that we work in him and he in us.'[12] Pope Paul VI seemed to echo these sentiments when he wrote, 'The techniques of evangelisation are valuable ... But the most careful preparation by a preacher will be of no avail without the Holy Spirit and no discourse will be capable of moving people's hearts unless it is inspired by him. Without him the most skilful plans of sociologists will prove valueless.'[13] Surely these words are of crucial importance in the contemporary Church.

Only a vivid experience of saving faith can provide people engaged in mission or ministry of any kind, with both the desire and the power to witness to the good news of God's unconditional love, with courage, conviction, credibility and consistency. The extent to which it is lacking, is the extent to which the well-intentioned efforts of people like priests in pulpits, teachers in classrooms and parents in homes, will fail to bear fruit.

The kerygmatic proclamation has to be demonstrated in deeds of mercy and compassion. As Paul said, it is a matter of 'faith expressing itself through love.'(Gal 5:5) While there are countless ways of doing this, I'd suggest that the following four are important. Firstly, by forgiving those who have caused us hurt or injury.[14] Secondly, by working for reconciliation between churches and between people within churches. Thirdly, by engaging in works of charity which benefit people, especially the poor, marginalised and the victims of oppression. Fourthly, by engaging in action for justice by identifying and changing those structures of society which tend to perpetuate systemic forms of evil.

Philanthropic action of any kind, which may appear to be good in itself, can be rooted in conscious or unconscious motives such as guilt, a need to be needed, a desire to create a good impression, unacknowledged feelings of inferiority, envious anger, etc. The extent to which it fails to be the expression of an awareness of God's unrestricted love, is the extent to which it will fail to have any real Christian significance as a form of witness. As Pope Paul VI has reminded us, 'The people of our day are more impressed by witness than by teachers, and if they listen to these, it is because they also bear witness.'[15]

Trusting Faith

Trusting faith empowers us to do God's will, no matter how difficult or impossible it might seem to be. If we present the five loaves and two fish of our good intentions, the Lord, by his grace, will bless whatever efforts we are able to make. By doing so, he enables us to be effective in our Christian lives and ministries.

Trusting faith is sustained by the conviction that 'God is able to do immeasurably more can we can ask or imagine, according to his power that is at work within us.'(Eph 3:20) The power of God can be experienced in three ways. Firstly, it *strengthens* us in our weakness, thereby blessing our efforts on the Lord's behalf. Secondly, it *provides* for us in all our needs. Instead of worrying about personal inadequacies or worldly obstacles, we rely on the sustaining power and providence of him who cares for the birds of the air and clothes the lilies of the field. Thirdly, it not only *assures* us that the Lord can and does draw good from the evil that afflicts our lives, it can help us to overcome the perverse and perverting power that we call the devil. We will reflect on each of these points in turn.

The faith that gives strength

Once we can say with St Paul, 'I live by faith in the Son of God, who loved me and gave himself for me,'(Gal 2:20) we realise that in everyday events we are called by God to, 'live by faith and not by sight.'(2 Cor 5:7) It seems to me that this involves two interrelated things.

To begin with, we need to seek God's will in all the circumstances of daily life and to be guided in all things by his Spirit. We exercise trusting faith when we ask God 'to fill us with the knowledge of his will through all spiritual wisdom and understanding.'(Col 1:9) As the apostle James once wrote, 'Ask (for this spiritual perception) in faith, never doubting ... for the doubter, being double minded and unstable in every way, must not expect to receive anything from the Lord.'(Jas 1:6-9) God can reveal his will to us in one of many different ways, e.g. an inner prompting associated with the consolation of the Spirit, a scripture text, providential circumstances, etc.[16]

Secondly, having received guidance from the Lord, we exercise trusting faith by believing that he will empower us to do what he has inspired us to do. As St Paul assures us in Phil 2:13, 'God is at work in you to will and to act according to his good purpose.'

Like many others I have suffered from what psychologists call performance anxiety. It even surfaces in my dreams. For example, I sometimes see myself about to preach to a congregation when I suddenly realise that the microphone is dead. With mounting fear I fiddle with switches and plugs in a desperate effort to restore power before the people get fed up and leave the church in frustration. It raises the question, whose power do I depend on in my work, my own or that of the Lord?

A few years ago I had to face this kind of dilemma in reality. We were conducting a mission in a Dublin parish. I wasn't feeling well as I was suffering from high levels of stress and emotional fatigue. On one of the days – it happened to be my fortieth birthday – I was relieved to find that I was neither the appointed preacher nor celebrant for that night. However, a few moments before the eucharist was due to begin I was asked to preside for reasons I cannot now remember. What I do recall is the feeling of powerlessness and emptiness I felt. Standing at the vesting bench I said a quiet prayer under my breath, 'Lord I am at the end of my tether. I am completely drained. I have nothing to offer. How can I lead your people in the *celebration* of the eucharist? Unless you help me, my efforts will be in vain.'

With that, we processed on to the sanctuary and the mass began. After a colleague delivered the homily, I approached the altar to begin the offertory prayers. Once again a feeling of powerlessness came over me. I silently repeated the words I had expressed in the sacristy, and proceeded with the blessing of the gifts. As I read the eucharistic prayer something happened. I became palpably aware of a mysterious presence. I was so moved by this consoling experience that for a moment I couldn't speak. During the pause I was amazed to find that there was an uncanny silence in the Church. There wasn't a sound. No one was coughing, shuffling or rustling paper. Evidently, everyone was aware of the presence. When I regained my composure, I said, 'I'm sure you can all sense it. The Holy Spirit has come upon all of us, the risen Lord is here.' As I continued with the Mass the sense of presence deepened. It was one of the most wonderful spiritual experiences of my life.

When the eucharist ended, there were unusually long queues outside the confession boxes. When people came in they said such things as, 'What on earth happened out there tonight? ... That was the happiest half hour I have ever experienced in my life ... I wish it could have gone on and on ... I feel that God has taken away many of my fears and given me his peace instead.'

What a paradox! When I was at my lowest ebb from a human point of view, I was granted one of the greatest blessings of my entire priestly ministry. Besides being the best birthday present I ever received, it taught me a number of things. If we are seeking to follow God's will, and to minister in his name, there is no need to be afraid. If we trust in his goodness and love, we discover that his 'grace is sufficient for us, for his power is made perfect in weakness ... I can do everything through him who gives me strength.'(2 Cor

12:9; Phil 4:13) Nowadays, when I face similar crucifixion points of powerlessness in my life and ministry, instead of anxiously wrestling with my fears, I try to prayerfully nestle in the Lord through faith. As a result, I find that I am increasingly sustained by the conviction that, 'the Lord blesses those who put their trust in him.'(Jer 17:7)

Faith that God will provide
Besides relying on God's power to strengthen them in weakness, people with trusting faith are convinced that, if they concentrate on trying to carry out God's will, somehow or other, in a non-magical way, he will provide. As Jesus promised, 'Strive first for the kingdom of God and his righteousness, and all else will be added to you as well.' (Mt 6:33)

I experienced the truth of our Lord's words when I was on retreat in London a few years ago. On the evening of the second day, one of my brothers phoned me to say that our mother had just died unexpectedly in Dublin. He also mentioned that we were facing a practical problem. Another of our brothers was in France or Spain on a camping holiday, so there was no way of contacting him to tell him either about mum's death or the funeral arrangements. The question arose, would we delay the funeral for ten days until he returned, or go ahead without him?

I went to the chapel in a state of shock. As I knelt before the tabernacle in tears, a line from morning prayer in the Divine Office drifted into my mind. Some words from the book of Job had made a strong impression on me. 'Naked I came from my mother's womb, and naked I shall return. The Lord gives, the Lord takes away, blessed be the name of the Lord ... If we accept happiness from the Lord's hands, must we not accept sorrow also?'(Job 1:21) I felt a strong sense of identification with these sentiments. Immediately, I decided to accept God's will by offering my mother back to him in a prayer of sincere thanksgiving. It had a paradoxical effect. Although I still felt shocked and sorrowful at one level of awareness, at another I felt strangely at peace. Now that I was without an earthly mum or dad, I felt a consoling sense of closeness to God, my heavenly parent, so to speak.

In the light of that experience, I began to think about the issue of my mother's funeral. It struck me that we couldn't wait until my brother returned from holidays. Then I wondered what my mother would have wanted herself. I got a strong feeling that she would have desired my brother to be there, not for her sake, but because it would be good for him. I also had a growing impression that this would also be the loving will of God. As Jesus once said, 'If you parents, bad and all as you are, know how to give good gifts to your children, how much more will your Father in heaven give you whatever you ask of him?'(Mt 7:11) So I said to him, 'Heavenly Father, I need your help. With confidence in your repeated promises to answer prayer, I thank you that somehow or other you will use circumstances – even apparently unfortunate ones – to bring my brother back to the funeral on time.' As I said this prayer, I had a quiet conviction that all would be well.

When I returned from London we tried to contact my brother, in the belief that God helps those who try to help themselves. But all to no avail. No one knew where he was. I wasn't really worried. We brought mum's remains to the church, and still there was no word. Then around eleven that night the phone rang. It was a friend of my brother's in London. Providentially, as it turned out, we had been in touch with him earlier in the day to see if he knew anything. 'You won't believe this,' he said, 'but your brother called here earlier this evening. Apparently one of his children was involved in a minor accident. She is perfectly OK now, but your sister-in-law got such a fright that she decided to return home immediately. I have given your brother the sad news of your mother's death and he is trying to make it to the boat at Holyhead tonight.' For my part, I felt pretty sure that he would.

Next morning we set off for the Church. There was still no sign of my brother. As I came out on the sanctuary to begin requiem mass, a side door opened, and in walked my brother and sister-in-law. Once again I felt consoled and strengthened by a strong sense of God's closeness and love in the midst of vulnerability and sorrow. I hadn't trusted him in vain. He had been true to his promise to answer the prayer of faith. In his providence he had helped the family at its crucifixion point of powerlessness by using what looked like an unfortunate incident to bless us all.

The whole episode taught me as never before that if we focus conscientiously on trying to do God's loving will to the best of our ability, we can trust him to supply whatever is lacking. When one reads the lives of saintly men and women who have accomplished great things for God, one invariably finds that they were inspired and sustained by this kind of faith. When Cecil Kerr, of the Christian Renewal Centre in Rostrevor, and Sister Consilio, of the Cuan Mhuire rehabilitation Centres, were embarking on their respective projects, they had to rely on God's providence.[17] This sense of dependence not only informed their efforts, it gave them the assurance that God would supply whatever was lacking. As each of them dedicated themselves to following God's will in a spirit of trust, the money and material things they needed simply came their way, sometimes in the most remarkable circumstances. It seems to me that only those who have trusting faith in the providence of God, dream dreams and see visions that translate into audacious action of a practical and fruitful kind.

The assurance that God will overcome evil
Over the years I have come to appreciate that there is another type of trusting faith. Like our forebears, we ourselves, and the people we care about, will become the victims of all kinds of misfortune. As Barbara Ward and Rene Dubos have written, 'The actual life of most of mankind has been cramped with back-breaking labour, exposed to deadly or debilitating disease, prey to wars and famines, haunted by the loss of children, filled with fear and the ignorance that breeds more fear. At the end, for everyone, stands dreaded unknown death.'[18] Besides these external evils, there are also our own weaknesses and sins. It is important that we look at evil of all kinds from the point of view of our faith in God, rather than looking at faith in God from the point of view of evil. The latter approach tends to weaken our confidence in the Lord, whereas the former strengthens the conviction that, no matter what form evil takes, it will never have the last word. Since the victorious death of Jesus on the cross, that word belongs to God. He can bring good out of all

the evil circumstances of our lives. They are embraced and transcended by his plan of salvation. The Easter liturgy acknowledges this fact when, speaking of original sin and its disastrous effects, it says, 'Oh happy fault, O necessary sin, that won for us such a great Redeemer.' St Paul expressed the same triumphant faith when he wrote, 'God has imprisoned all in disobedience so that he may be merciful to all ... where sin abounds, there the grace of God more abounds.'(Rom 11:32)

We can no more rid the world of evil than an oyster can rid itself of the grit that has entered its inner life. But just as the oyster can transform an alien presence by forming a beautiful pearl around it, so the Lord can transform the presence of evil in our lives by the all-embracing action of his grace. Paradoxically, the greater the evil, the greater the pearl that is finally revealed.(cf Mt 13:45) Pope John Paul I had this notion in mind when he said, 'I run the risk of making a blunder, but I will say it: The Lord loves humility so much that sometimes he allows serious sins. Why? In order that those who committed these sins may, after repenting, remain humble. One does not feel inclined to think oneself half a saint, half an angel, when one knows that one has committed serious faults.'[19] It was probably an intuition like this that inspired St Paul to say, 'Give thanks in *all circumstances* for this is the will of Christ Jesus for you.'(1 Thess 5:18) We thank God not *for* all circumstances, e.g. cancer, alcoholism, marital infidelity, a moral weakness, premature death, etc., but rather *in* all circumstances. We do this at all our crucifixion points of powerlessness in the firm belief that, somehow or other, God will finally bring good out of evil, either in this life or in the next. As scripture assures us, 'all things work for good with those who love God and put their faith in him.'(cf Rm 8:28) If our mission and ministry are informed by this kind of trusting faith, we will tend to engender Christian hope in the hearts of those we are called to serve. As G K Chesterton wrote in his Ballad of the White Horse, 'Those marked with the cross of Christ go gaily in the dark.'

In our daily lives we all of us have to contend with the mystery of evil that is called the devil. It can impinge upon our own lives, the lives of people we care about and upon the structures of church and state. Hans Kung has written, 'Certainly the power of evil, as it finds expression in all its menace in the life and death of Jesus, should not be minimised even today ... In the light of both the New Testament ('principalities and powers') and of modern sociological conclusions ('anonymous powers and systems'), evil as power is essentially more than the sum total of the wickedness of individuals.'[20]

I used to sense this kind of evil in a recurring dream. I'd feel threatened by an insidious presence that was so terrifying that it would leave me speechless. I'd anxiously think to myself, 'If only I could say the name of Jesus, this evil would go away.' Then I would struggle to utter the Holy Name. At first, I would only manage to whisper it with difficulty. Then I'd be able to say it. When finally, I could shout it out with defiant conviction, the sense of evil would evaporate completely. The same is true in our waking hours. The Lord can deliver us from evil, not necessarily the kind that can kill the body, but the kind that can end up as Jesus said, 'with the body and soul being destroyed in hell.'(Mt 10:28) As the scriptures assure us, 'The one who is in you, (i.e. the Spirit of God) is greater than the one who is in the world (i.e. Satan).'(1 Jn 4:4) No matter what temptation comes our way, we can learn to resist by relying, in our crucifixion points of powerlessness, on the name and the power of the Lord.(cf 1 Cor 10:13) This kind of faith becomes a spiritual shield that 'quenches *all* the fiery darts of the evil one.'(Eph 6:16)

While most of the problems we encounter in pastoral ministry are merely human, e.g. of a psychological, social or economic nature, occasionally they are due to spiritual oppression of an unusual kind. If we discern that 'Our struggle is not against enemies of blood and flesh,'(Eph 6:12), we can trust the promise of him who said, 'These signs of power will accompany those who believe; by using my name they will cast out demons.'(Mk 16:17) It authorises Christian men and women, who have discerned the presence of an evil spirit, to perform simple as opposed to solemn exorcisms. As St Alphonsus Liguori points out, 'private exorcism is lawful to all Christians.'[21] Solemn exorcism, on the other hand, is rightly reserved to someone appointed by the bishop.[22] So whenever we suspect that a person's problem involves more than a psychological pathology, we can silently pray in words like, 'In the name of Jesus Christ, unholy spirit, I command you to depart from this creature of God.' In my experience, both in and out of the sacrament of penance, such a prayer of deliverance can be effective if it is prudently offered in a spirit of expectant faith.[23] It is uttered in the knowledge, as Paul says, that we do not wage war according to human standards, 'for the weapons of our warfare are not merely human, but they have power to destroy strongholds (of evil) and every proud obstacle raised against the knowledge of God.'(cf 1 Cor 10:4-6)

Charismatic Faith

Besides the saving and trusting forms of faith which we have already examined, there is a third type which can be referred to as charismatic, or mountain-moving faith. Whereas all Christians need to have the first two sorts of faith, if they are to grow in holiness, they do not need the charismatic variety in order to do so. Indeed St Fulgentius wrote,[24] 'The Holy Spirit can confer all kinds of gifts (e.g. the charism of faith) without being present himself.' Normally, however, the charism is granted by God to those who are already exercising saving and trusting faith in their lives. Like any extraordinary gift of the Spirit, it is only entrusted to some members of the Christian community. They receive it on behalf of the entire body and have a responsibility to use it humbly for the upbuilding of individuals and the Church. [25]

The charism of faith is mentioned by Paul in 1 Cor 12:9 and again in 1 Cor 13:2. He indicates that it is the key to exercising what can be called the gifts of power, such as the ability to heal the sick, perform miracles and to drive out evil spirits. They are the good news in action with an ability, in the words of Paul VI, to 'win the attention and astonishment of the profane and secularised world.'[26] The apostle Paul said that his preaching did not depend on arguments drawn from human philosophy but on a 'demonstration of the Spirit and power.'(1 Cor 2:4) Writing about this unusual kind of faith, St Cyril of Jerusalem explained to his catechumens,[27] 'Charismatic faith, in the sense of a particular divine grace conferred by the Spirit, is not primarily concerned with doctrine but with giving people powers which are quite beyond their capability. The person who has this kind of faith will say to the mountain, "move from here to there," and it will move, and anyone who can in fact say these words through faith, and believe without hesitation that they will come to pass, receives this particular grace.' Writing about the charisms of faith and power mentioned in 1 Cor 12, St Thomas states that the preacher of the gospel should preach as Jesus did, confirming the message either through healings and miracles or by living such a holy life that can be explained only by the power of the Spirit. If we preach the power of Jesus to save and redeem the whole person, people want to see that power made real.[28] I believe that this point particularly relevant in an age of transition when people in a secular culture find it hard to believe.

Jesus on the charism of faith

It has often occurred to me, while reading the gospels, that it was usually the charism of faith that Jesus commended in the lives of people he met. Scripture scholars seem to confirm this impression. Gunther Borkman has written, 'There can be do doubt that the faith which Jesus demands, and which alone he recognises as such, has to do with power and with miracle.'[29] Norman Perrin seconds this opinion when he writes, 'Many of the most characteristic sayings about faith in the gospels are associated with miracles, especially healing miracles, and critical scholarship has found this aspect of the tradition very difficult.'[30] For example, when the centurion asked Jesus to help his dying servant, he showed remarkable faith when he said, 'Lord I am not worthy to have you come under my roof, but only speak the word and my servant will be healed.' Jesus was so impressed by the soldier's unquestioning confidence in his ability to heal, that he exclaimed, 'Truly I tell you, in no one in Israel have I found such faith.'(Mt 8:8;10)

On more than one occasion, Jesus admonished the apostles for their lack of this kind of faith. For example, when the storm blew up on the lake and the apostles were scared of sinking, they roused their sleeping companion, 'Lord, save us!' they cried, 'We are perishing!'(Mt 8:25) With magisterial authority, Jesus calmed the sea with a word, and turning to the apostles he said, 'Why are you afraid, you of little faith?' Not content with the saving and trusting faith they had desperately exercised, he evidently expected them to have such confident belief in God that it would have amounted to the charism of faith. If they had exercised that particular gift, they themselves would have been able to say to the wind and waves, 'In the name of the Lord, be still, be calm.'

Jesus spoke about the need for charismatic faith and also about it's nature. For example, when the apostles, unlike their master, failed to exorcise a young boy, they asked, 'Why could we not cast it out?' to which Jesus replied, 'Because of your little faith. For truly, I tell you, if you have faith the size of a mustard seed, you will say to this mountain, "Move from here to there," and it will move; and nothing will be impossible for you.'(Mt 17:19-22) Another time Jesus cursed a fig tree which had failed to bear fruit. The following morning when Peter drew attention to the fact that it had withered overnight, the Lord replied, 'Have faith in God.' Apparently a more literal translation would read, 'Have God's faith,' i.e. the special gift that only God can give. Then straightaway he went on to say, 'Truly I tell you, if you say to this mountain, "Be taken up and thrown into the sea," and *do not doubt in your heart*, but believe that what you say will come to pass, it will be done for you. So I tell you, whatever you ask for in prayer, *believe that you have received it*, and it will be yours.'(Mk 11:22-25) A number of points can be made about this astounding promise of Jesus.

Characteristics of charismatic faith
Firstly, we will have faith in God's promises to the extent that we have faith in the God of the promises. Through saving and trusting faith we learn what the Father is like. We recognise that he loves us so much that he would want to bless us. As St Paul said, 'If God has given us his Son, would he not give us all things in him?'(Rom 8:32) He is the one who in his boundless generosity says to us, 'All I have is yours.'(Lk 15:31) Jesus referred to this intuitive awareness of God's loving impulses when he said, 'If you who are evil know how to give good gifts to your children, how much more will the Father in heaven give good gifts to those who ask him?'(Mt 7:11)

Secondly, as far as I am aware, there is only one place in the scriptures where we are told how the different kinds of faith can grow. 'Faith,' as we have already noted, 'comes by hearing the word of God.'(Rom 10:17) What St Paul is referring too here is either a particular word of revelation that jumps off the page of scripture, alive into the heart, or what charismatics call a 'word of knowledge,' i.e. a gratuitous hunch or insight of an intuitive kind. Like the proverbial two edged sword, it is alive and active, going where no other word can go, 'to judge the secret thoughts and emotions of the heart.'(Heb 4:12) In whatever way it comes, it evokes the mustard seed of inner certainty that is characteristic of charismatic faith, while providing the power to do what it says.(cf Is 55:11) There is an example of such an empowering word in Matthew's account of how Jesus walked on the water.

At first the apostles were terrified when they saw the Lord. 'Take courage!' he said, 'It is I. Don't be afraid.' Then Peter, who realised that trusting faith wasn't enough in the circumstances, replied, 'Lord, if it is you, tell me to come to you.' It is then that Jesus spoke the single word that could evoke mountain-moving faith, when he said to Peter, 'Come.' As long as Peter relied solely and entirely on Jesus and his word, he could walk on water. But as soon as he began to focus on gravity, wind and waves, he started to sink. As a result, he lost the grace of the present moment, regressed to trusting faith, and had to cry out, 'Lord, save me!' Having reached out to rescue him, Jesus admonished Peter for his lack of charismatic faith. 'You of little faith,' he exclaimed, 'why did you doubt?'(Mt 14:22-34) It seems to me that he might want to ask his modern day disciples much the same question.(cf Mt 17:17)

Thirdly, people with trusting faith of the non-charismatic kind, believe that the promises of Christ are true with their *minds*. But in everyday situations, e.g. praying for a relative suffering from cancer, they find it hard to trust the promises with their *hearts*. As the late Kathryn Kuhlman, who was well known for her remarkable healing ministry, once said, 'There are many who mix the ingredients of their own mental attitude with a little confidence, a little pinch of trust, a generous handful of religious egoism, quote some

Scripture, add some desire – then mix it all together and label it faith ... We have formed the habit of trying to appropriate by belief, forgetting that belief is mental – faith is from God ... Faith as God himself imparts to the heart is spiritual. It's warm. It's vital. It lives. It throbs. Its power is absolutely irresistible when it is imparted to the heart by the Lord.'[31] Trusting faith of the non-charismatic kind prays in the *hope* that God *may* do something in the *future, if* what is asked is in accordance with his will. It is hedged about with ifs, buts and caveats. Significantly, Jesus never said to anyone, 'Your *hope* has saved you or made you well!'

Heartfelt faith, of the charismatic kind that Jesus admired, is so sure of God's promises that it prays with the *conviction* that the Lord *is* doing something in the *present*. This kind of faith is clearly adverted to in 1 Jn 5:14, when he states, 'This is the confidence we have in God, that if we ask anything according to his will, he hears us. And if we know he hears us in whatever we ask, we know *we have obtained* the requests made of him.' Instead of having to see evidence in order to believe, this kind of faith believes in order to see. It's future hope is rooted in present conviction. As the letter to the Hebrews puts it, 'Faith is the assurance (in the present) of things hoped for (in the future), the conviction (in the present) of things not seen (in the future).'(Heb 11:1) As Derek Prince has pointed out, 'Hopes that are based on true faith in the heart will not be disappointed. But without this basis there is no assurance that our hopes will be fulfilled.'[32]

Fourthly, it is clear that people are only empowered to pray or to act with charismatic faith in so far as they consciously do so in accord with God's will. What is involved here is an immediate, intuitive rapport with what God wants, rather than some abstract or notional conception of the will of the Lord. To exercise charismatic faith, Christians need to develop a growing sensitivity to the nuances and subtleties of the Spirit's guidance in the concrete, here and now circumstances of life and ministry. I have dealt elsewhere with this all-important subject.[33]

For example, a nun rang recently. She asked if she could bring one of her companions to see me because she was suffering from a chronic back complaint. I reluctantly agreed. When they arrived, the sister who had arranged the meeting explained that as I preached at a conference a week or so previously, she had become convinced that if I prayed for her friend, she would recover. For my part, I was very sceptical. I suspected that it was a case of wishful thinking. But as I listened to the sister speak with such obvious compassion about the woman with the bad back, I had a growing sense that her desire for healing seemed to have been prompted by the Spirit, and was therefore, a manifestation of God's will.

As I encountered what was yet another crucifixion point of powerlessness, I had an inner conviction – though not a strong one – that the sister could recover. As a result of many such experiences I would say, in retrospect, that my level of conviction would only have scored a five on a scale of one to ten. There have been other occasions when I would have given such an inner conviction a score of eight or nine out of ten. In any case, I felt on this occasion that I should administer the Sacrament of the Sick. As St James promised, 'Are any among you sick? They should call the elders of the church and have them pray over them, anointing them with oil in the name of the Lord. The prayer of *faith* (charismatic faith) *will* save the sick, and the Lord will raise them up.'(Jas 5:14-16)

To cut a longer story short, I anointed the sister with the bad back. As I did so I felt that the Lord was indeed working within her, planting seeds of healing grace that would bear fruit in the days to come. Thank God they did. Two weeks later the person who had been anointed phoned me to say that her back was much better. All the pain was gone and her ability to bend backwards, forwards and sideways had returned. There was reason to believe that she, like many others, had been healed. I can say in passing that I have often been disappointed to find that some priests only expect the sacrament of anointing to enable people to bear with their suffering as a share in the suffering of Christ. They don't really expect it to bring about healing of mind or body. In the light of this lack of faith, is it any wonder that many of the faithful resort to dubious alternatives of the New Age variety?

Conclusion

All of us need to grow in faith. It enables us to appropriate in conscious experience the grace of salvation which we first received in
baptism. It is this awareness of the loving kindness of the heart of
our God, that gives us the ability to witness to the good news.
Trusting faith strengthens us in this on-going task. It also assures
us that God will provide for our material needs, no matter what obstacle we encounter in trying to show his mercy and love in the
wider community. Finally, while we grow in saving and trusting
faith, God may choose to bless us from time to time with the charism of faith. As St Cyril of Jerusalem said, 'In so far as it depends on
you, cherish the gift of saving faith which leads you to God and you
will then receive the higher gift which no effort of yours can reach,
no powers of yours attain.' [34]

Even a mustard seed of this gift will assure us in our crucifixion
points of powerlessness, that if we act or pray in the name of Jesus,
the mighty promises he made to the apostles will be fulfilled in our
lives. 'Very truly, I tell you, the one who believes in me *will also do
the works I do*, and in fact, will do greater works than these, because
I am going to the Father. *I will do whatever you ask in my name*, so that
the Father may be glorified in the Son. If in my name you ask me for
anything I will do it.'(Jn 14:12-15) It seems to me that contemporary
forms of mission and ministry will be effective to the extent that
they are expressions of saving, trusting and charismatic faith, for
'without (such) faith it is impossible to please God.'(Heb 11:6)

As we come to the end of the twentieth century, it is clear that our
pluralistic and secularised culture is presenting the Church with a
tremendous challenge. Unfortunately, it seems at times that many
Christians are weak in faith. They sometimes settle for defensive
maintenance rather than engaging in enthusiastic mission. So instead of gaining new members, the Church is losing many of the
members it already has, especially in deprived urban areas. This is
a sad and ironic fact when one considers that Jesus came, as he said
himself, 'to bring the good news to the poor'(Lk 4:18)

Significantly, the only Christian groups who seem to be expanding in numbers and influence at the moment appear to be those who believe in what John Wimber calls 'power evangelism.'[35] The others believe in what he calls 'presence evangelism.' It stresses the importance of incarnating faith by inculturating the good news, performing works of mercy, and taking action to achieve social justice. While accepting the importance of this approach, evangelical, charismatic and pentecostal groups stress the primary need for an active proclamation of the good news which is also backed up by deeds of power such as occasional healings and miracles. While I would have some reservations about the political conservatism, the intellectual fundamentalism and the supernaturalistic tendencies of these approaches to evangelisation, it seems to me that we have a lot to learn from them. Rightly, they stress the all-important role of heartfelt faith of a saving, trusting *and* charismatic kind.

And so, with them and the first disciples, we pray in this the decade of evangelisation: 'Now Lord, consider the threats we are facing and enable your servants to speak your word with great boldness. Stretch out your hand to heal and to perform miraculous signs and wonders through the name of your holy servant Jesus.' (Acts 4:29-30) As the Lord answers this prayer anew, perhaps many crows will end up singing sweetly like blackbirds, for 'what is impossible for mortals is possible for God.'(Lk 18:27)

Notes

1   *Dynamics of Faith*, NY, Harper & Row, 1957, p 1.

2   *Two Types of Faith*, NY, Harper & Row, 1961.

3   *Faith and Belief*, NJ, Princeton, 1979.

4   *Stages of Faith*, San Francisco, Harper & Row, 1981.

5   'The Absence of God in Modern Culture' in *Second Collection*, Ed Ryan & Tyrell, Philadelphia, The Westminster Press, 1974, pp 101-116.

6   *The Faith that Does Justice*, Ed J. C. Haughey, NY, Paulist Press, 1972.

7   In his *Apostolic Preaching and its Development*, and *The Essential Nature of New Testament Preaching*, C H Dodd maintains that an examination of 1 Cor 15 and the speeches in Acts shows that the kerygma normally contained the following six points:
1. The age of fulfilment has dawned: the Old Testament prophesies have been realised; the hope of Israel is now present in fact.
 2. This fulfilment is shown by the life, death and resurrection of Jesus the Messiah.
3. In virtue of the resurrection he is exalted as Lord.
4. The Holy Spirit's presence in the church is a token of God's favour toward his people.
 5. Christ will come again as Judge and Saviour.
 6. There is an appeal for repentance, an offer of forgiveness and the gift of the Holy Spirit, and an assurance of salvation.

8   *Maturing in the Spirit* , Dublin, Columba, 1991, pp 34-36 .

9   Billy Graham, 'The Holy Spirit and Salvation,' in *The Holy Spirit*, London, Fount, 1980, pp 59-60.

10   *The Call to Conversion* , Herts., Lion, 1986, esp pp 18-38.

11   cf Code of Canon Law, No 849.

12   P. Coste, Ed, *Saint Vincent de Paul: Correspondence, Entretiens, Documents* Vol. XI 342.

13   *Evangelisation Today*, par 75.

14   See P. Collins, 'Forgiveness and Healing' in *Growing in Health and Grace*, Galway, Campus, 1991.

15   *Evangelisation Today*, par 41.

16   See P. Collins, 'Be guided by the Spirit' in *Maturing in the Spirit.*

17   Cecil Kerr, *The Way of Peace: Peace Amidst the Conflict of Northern Ireland*, London, Hodder & Stoughton, 1990; Gemma Costello *In God's Hands: A Story of Sr Consilio and Cuan Muire*, Dublin, Veritas, 1985.

18   *Only One Earth* , London, Pelican, 1972, p 35.

19 General Audience, 6th Sept 1978.

20 *Eternal Life*, London, Fount, 1985, p 167.

21 J. Mc Manus, 'Exorcism in Catholic Moral Theology' in *Deliverance Prayer*, Ed M & D Linn, NY, Paulist Press, 1981, pp 242-251.

22 Code of Canon Law, 1172.1.

23 For more on this see P Collins, 'Exorcism and the Falling Phenomenon' in *Maturing in the Spirit*, chap 10.

24 *Contra Fabianum*, Fragment 28; PL 65, 791.

25 Abbott, 'The Church' in *Documents of Vatican II*, par 12.

26 E. D. O'Connor, Ed, *Pope Paul and the Spirit*, Notre Dame, Ave Maria Press, 1978.

27 Cat 5, 10-11, Readings, week 31, Wed, *The Divine Office*, Vol 3.

28 cf 'Healing and the Priesthood' by Frank McNutt, *New Covenant*, Nov 1979.

29 *Jesus of Nazareth*, NY, Harper & Row, 1930, p 131.

30 *Rediscovering the Teaching of Jesus*, NY, Harper & Row, 1967, p 15.

31 'Faith' in *A glimpse into Glory*, NJ, Logos, 1979, p 45.

32 'Faith vs Hope' in *Faith to Live By*, Ann Arbor, CGM/Servant, 1977, p 23.

33 'Be Guided by the Spirit' in *Maturing in the Spirit*, 1990, and 'Praying for Healing' sec 3, pp 96-112 & 130-134.

34 Cat 5-10, *op cit*.

35 *Power Evangelism*, London, Hodder & Stoughton, 1985, and *Power Healing*, London, Hodder & Stoughton, 1986.

PART II

New Beginnings in Ministry

Who Is in Charge of the Playground?

Robert Whiteside

The creaking clerical bones bend down and scoop up the folded piece of paper. Opening it delicately, he notices that the folds are almost worn through. It's a restaurant bill:

THE WILLOW GROVE

Dinner for two	£20.40
Wine	£10.00
Total	£30.40
Service charge 10%	£03.40
	£33.80

It seems old – faded and brown at the edges – like it had been in the man's wallet for a long time, maybe ten years. About to screw it up in a ball and throw it in the waste- paper basket, he stops himself and looks at it again, noticing the faded biro writing that scrawled the message £33.80. Feeling the delicate texture of the paper, rubbed to smoothness by years of pocketing, he realizes that this is not just another restaurant bill. This is a treasure. It has been kept for a reason. It must have fallen from the man's wallet when he had been groping for the mass offering.

Reverently refolding it he places it behind the digital clock that pulses on the mantlepiece and whose regular blink reminds him to keep boundaries on his fifty-minute hour – a way of dealing with tardy visitors he had picked up from a therapist friend.

Glancing at it again, the frayed edges peeking poignantly from behind the clock catch his eye. There is a sort of timelessness about it in contrast to the bleeping colon of the digital face, relentlessly reminding him that time is passing him by. It looks out of place – almost lonely. It reminds him of an occasion he found a love-worn teddy bear, obviously dropped by an unwary child, lying on a deserted railway station platform. Momentarily, his eyes moist over. Crossing over to the mantlepiece again, he gingerly extracts it from behind the clock, opens it gently, and holds it in his open palms with a very definite reverence. There is a sacredness about this document. All of a sudden he feels guilty about even looking at it, as if he is reading a private love letter. But then maybe he is. There is certainly something symbolic about it. Gazing more through it than at it, he begins to paint imaginary scenarios in his mind, only vaguely aware of the fire toasting his left mid-shin:

> … It had been her fortieth birthday and they had celebrated at this little hideaway place. He had bought her 40 heart-shaped chocolates, a necklace with 40 pearls (not real), and, encouraged by her playful protests, kissed her forty times in the car park before they came in. They had laughed and cried. It was the night that gave rise to their pet names - she had become 'Willow' and he 'Grover.'

> … 'Twas the night of her mother's funeral. He had noticed her growing weary of the well-meaning mourners, lied to them about having to visit Aunt Joan, slipped her into the car and whisked her off for a late night meal. For a long time she had stared at the centrepiece candle and said in a monotone, 'I'm glad she's gone.' It seemed to help her.

> … Perhaps it was the night he had forgotten to bring money and she had to drink endless cups of coffee while he drove home for what became known as his 'Willow Card.'

> … Then there was the night they got the giggles at the waiter with an affected posh accent who kept referring to her as 'Modom.' She had laughed so much that the tears made her mascara run. He had nicknamed her 'Weepie Willow.'

He could go on in this playful pursuit of interlacing his own intimate moments with the flights of fancy that the old bill arouses in
him, but the increasing heat of the fire is making its presence felt on
his left leg. Slipping the bill back to its lonely, temporary resting
place, he moves away from the fire. Funny, he has never met this
man before. Yet he knows about his pain, anger, neurosis, sexual
hangups, whatever. And somehow he feels he has entered into the
mystery of the man that is symbolised in that old bill. Anyway,
how can anyone explain the many layers of relational nuances that
lie hidden in that flimsy bit of paper? People can hazard guesses,
but only those involved can plumb the mystery.

* * *

The greatest objection brought against Christianity in our time,
and the real source of the distrust which insulates entire blocks
of humanity from the influence of the Church, has nothing to do
with historical or theological difficulties. It is the suspicion that
our religion makes its followers inhuman. *Teilhard de Chardin* [1]

Humanity and Christianity are incompatible in the minds of many.
The truth of de Chardin's point is being constantly borne out with
statements like, 'He's very human – not like a priest at all.' This
may well account for people's constant embarrassment and uneasi-
ness around the whole area of religion. For every anti-religious person I have met, I have encountered many more whose basic reaction to prayer, bible, spirituality, etc., is one of decided unease.
Official ministers have had to endure condemnation to cold, musty,
unused parlours, where they have been subjected to stilted quasi-
religious conversations, witnessed by grubby children who have
been corralled into a quiet resentful group in front of a switched-off
television. Frustrated by this kind of ministerial marginalisation,
some ministers have succumbed to frentic attempts to be chummy
by boning up on pop music, sport, and local politics. This contrived
attempt at 'humanising' oneself leads to further marginalisation
and feeling that one has donned the mantle of the stage vicar. Others
put the head down, switch off the emotions, quieten the critical
faculty, and work, work, work. Although this work centres around

people and their needs, gradually ministers find their humanity seeping away. Many could identify with Clinebell when he says, 'My life is characterised by a plethora of contacts and a poverty of relationships.'2

And work is precisely the issue – rather the obsession with work. The minister's dilemma is created by her tendency to view her role in life from the point of view of work. Her self-image is often that of the diligent worker in the field of the Lord who must not spare herself. This often means that she is regarded by others as a serious-minded individual intent upon bringing about change in people's lives. When she visits a home she is nearly always seen as calling with an agenda. Even before she has opened her mouth she is greeted with an excuse, 'Oh, hello ... I don't go to church,' 'I'm not a religious person, but I try to be kind to people,' 'I'm sorry the place is in a mess.' The frustration continues.

Perhaps one approach to this dilemma would be to let go of the work image and to use play as the model for ministerial activity. This would mean that he could begin to lay down the huge burden of responsibility many ministers grim-facedly carry around.

Although many attempts have been made at an exact definition of play, it has proved difficult to tie down. Robert K. Johnston captures the main aspects in his description:

> Play is an activity which is freely and spontaneously entered into. Play, to be play, must be entered into without outside purpose. Though not an end in itself, it can, nevertheless, have several consequences. Chief among these are the joy and release, the personal fulfillment, the remembering of our common humanity and the presentiment of the sacred, which the player sometimes experiences in and through the activity. 3

Play has nothing to do with indulging in idleness or adopting a frivolous approach to life. Rather, play is an attitude of mind, a way of viewing reality, that allows the minister to adopt a more contemplative attitude to his life and work. Play would seem to provide an ideal context for a ministry that it vital. It relieves the minister, firstly from that deadly seriousness of intent; secondly, from an over-responsible attitude to people; thirdly, from a compulsion to bring about change and, finally, a desperate desire for results and goals. The minister is freed up, is less driven and, therefore, is in a better position to provide that essential space for people which will prove accepting, challenging, and supportive. Play creates a pastoral playground where those who would serve the Church shift from being working ministers to being playing contemplatives.

Moving from a working model for ministry to a playful one requires a number of shifts in perspective:

Responsibile for – to – Responsible with
Change – to – Context for Change
Production – to – Presence.

Responsible for – to – Responsible with
The working minister often finds himself burdened by his ministry. Almost without thinking, he can easily slip in the tell-tale phrase 'my parish,' indicating only too well that he envisages his care as being all-embracing. Even though he makes every attempt to involve people, he can unwittingly operate from a 'Father knows best' mentality. The controlling attitude usually has its roots in fear – he finds it difficult to trust others because he does not trust himself. This results in people not being allowed to breathe, not trusted to make their own decisions, not encouraged to experiment. The people have to be protected, and instructed about everything.

The playing contemplative, on other hand, freed from the compulsion to appear strong and in charge, moves from being responsible for people to being responsible with them. He has imbued the spirit Clinebell so aptly describes, 'The most basic learning for anyone who hopes to establish any kind of helping relationship is that it is safe to be transparently real.'[4] Having gently faced the truth about himself, he is in the process towards freedom and growth, and is thus better equipped to be with others in their journey along the same path.

Change – to – Context for change
A misunderstanding of Mt 28:19-20, 'Go, make disciples of all nations,' tends to make people in ministry think that they are in the

business of changing people. The problem is people do not want to change, and will always resist change. And rightly so. To directly want to change people is an arrogant position and would seem to indicate that the changer considers himself to be holding the high moral ground. Unfortunately, the working minister often tends to take this very direct approach and talks about 'getting to the people.' Often this mentality arises from a need in the minister to feel relevant and important.

Change, of course, is vital for the growth of the human being, but the individual must make the decisions around the changes in his/her life. The role of the minister is the creation of the space, atmosphere, environment that is change-friendly. If he can concentrate his efforts on building a relational climate in the community, change will take care of itself – the people will see to that. Given the right climate people will always heal each other. The playful contemplative does not attempt to change people; he concentrates on the adaptation of the context in which people lead out their lives. For example, if he would like the liturgy to be more community based, he might well do nothing directly about it for a year. However, he knows well that the introduction of a cup of tea after Sunday mass could speak more about the eucharist assembly than ten talks on the subject. It takes a playing contemplate, free from the need for instant gratification, to realise this.

Production – to – Presence
As well as missing the point, the minister who focuses primarily on goals and results is destined for a lot of frustration. She is in danger of adopting an implementation mentality, i.e. taking on board a renewal progamme, excellent in itself, and deciding that it is good for the parish. This carries the obvious danger of taking on a programme lock, stock, and barrel and squeezing the local community into shape to fit the model. Adoption without adaptation. The tempation to manage the people, to find the ultimate community solution, to wrap everything up, is very strong and tempting to any weary minister. Eventually, tired of the ambiguities of pastoring, the endless loose ends, the continual sense of incompleteness, the minister can yearn to cry 'Get me a solution and be done with it.'

She could well listen to John V. Taylor:

> This problem/solution view of life is a distortion of reality as we actually experience it. The universe is not a vast examination paper. Frustration and evil and pain can't be packaged as problems, nor does happiness simply consist in eliminating them. Salvation is not the same as solution.[5]

Players, while they know that things have to be done, tend not to get fixated by goals and results. They can more easily go with the flow. They well understand Stephen Pattison when he says:

> Imaginative, intuitive and receptive knowledge is required to understand them (people), as well as knowledge of general principles. It is misguided to allow neat objective intellectual formulae or plans to obscure this, especially in the religious community where mystery should stand at the centre and not be subordinated to rationality. The objective analysis and measurement of causes and effects in caring situations can miss out badly on subjective and personal elements of great significance, not least those of religious experience itself.[6]

Playful contemplatives understand that real presence is the most healing thing in the world. Because they are deeply in touch with the mystery in life, they have the ability to vibrate and pulsate alongside people and thus make the Word flesh for them. They enflesh the real presence.

It really is all about the paschal mystery. That is centre piece of it all. That is what is truly relevant. Howard Clinebell puts it most eloquently: 'There is only one relevance; that is the relevance to the deep needs of people; to the places in their lives where they hurt, hope, curse, pray, hunger for meaning and significant relationships.'[7] The pashcal mystery is another name for it. Our task is the discovery of the pashcal mystery in the lives of people and often articulating it for them. It is a question of ferreting out and naming death/resurrection, sadness/joy, agony/ecstasy in the minutiae of people's lives:

* A plastic rosary interlacing arthritic fingers – paschal mystery.

* A furry toy curling around the cold steel frame of the hosptial bed – paschal mystery.

* A giggling honeymoon couple standing awkwardly in the hotel foyer, mustering up courage to book in for the night – paschal mystery.

* Tears in the maternal eye as her first-born glances back before launching out on his maiden voyage across the school playground – paschal mystery.

*Flies buzzing around the sun-baked cross on the grave of a forgotten missionary – paschal mystery.

* Shared Horlicks at bedtime since 1942 – pashcal mystery.

* Breaking of the Bread, Gathering the Eucharistic Assembly, Getting Mass – paschal mystery.

Uncovering the paschal mystery – it's a work for playing contemplatives, those who realise that 'laughter and tears lie at the heart of pastoral relationships.'[8]

* * *

'Mystery play ... playing with the mystery,' he thinks, poking the fire. Slumped into the large armchair, he gazes at the red caverns amidst the coals, and indulges his own Weeping Willow thoughts.

Notes

1   Pierre Teilhard de Chardin quoted in Stephen Pattison, *A Critique of Pastoral Care*, London, SCM, 1988, p 158.

2   Howard J. Clinebell, *Basic Types of Pastoral Counselling*, Nashville, Abingdon, 1966, p 15.

3   Robert K. Johnston, *The Christian at Play*, Grand Rapids, Eerdmans, 1983, p 34.

4   Clinebell, *Pastoral Counselling*, p 295.

5   John V. Taylor quoted in Pattison, *Pastoral Care*, p 139.

6   Pattison, *Pastoral Care*, p 139.

7   Clinebell, *Pastoral Counselling*, p 14.

8   Pattison, *Pastoral Care*, p 144.

Ministry Today
Possibilities for Change*

Moya Curran

Experience of change

When I joined the staff in All Hallows in 1970, *aggiornamento* was in full swing among certain prophetic people in the country but in the institutional Church the great awakening had scarcely begun. Nevertheless here in All Hallows I was amazed to find a very sophisticated approach to pastoral education already in existence. I had come from a background of teacher education to discover a methodology in place which involved taking a video out to schools, recording the students teaching, replaying the tape in a group setting, analysing and assessing the underlying theological concepts and planning for the next session. No other educational establishment in the country, secular or religious, had comparable facilities. At once I discovered the importance placed on the pastoral formation of the students even if, at that time, it was confined to the ministry of the school.

In the academic sphere, the principle of integration of theory and praxis was consciously subscribed to, though in practice this was limited to discovering innovative ways of translating theological themes such as revelation, grace, and ecclesiology into images and language which could be communicated in homilies, sacramental encounters, and pastoral visitation. Ability to communicate clearly and accurately got high priority. The scene has changed quite dramatically, for now all students entering the Institute can expect an integrated approach not only in the area of academics and pastoral but in experiencing an inter-disciplinary approach at every level of study.

* *The text of an address delivered in All Hallows on 3 February 1992.*

Where the process of change became most apparent was in structure shifts, from a form of administration which was hierarchical to a more democratic mode. The process of transformation was gradual. It was symbolised by a more community-style dining arrangement in the refectory, the professors climbed down from their dais to the floor to eat along side the students and share the same dinner menu. This was traumatic at the time and caused a measure of resistance and uncertainty, but more was to come. The student of today would have no concept of so clear-cut a hierarchical structure; there are now no titles or privileges and everyone is on first name terms.

Liturgical celebration diversified, and small groups took the place of large assembles. More inter-action began with the local Church, and the College liturgies were opened up to all. Then a traditional approach to discipline took a knock. Rules were turned into expectations, in the hope that student awareness would move from a focus on authority to the implications of personal responsibility. With the shift to personal responsibility there were growing pains and a need for the students to have a forum in which to process both inner and outer conflicts. Inter-personal groups became the place where it was safe to express anger, sadness or confusion. Human development, both personal and inter-personal, took on new significance.

At the same time, pastoral reflection was introduced to help the student deal with the impact of field placements. This very skilled and professional process revealed more to the student about himself than about his placement. Human development and pastoral reflection were added to an already well-established approach to spiritual formation.

What was emerging was that the person of the student had moved to centre stage and the formation process concentrated on the whole person. The concept of holistic education is at present most clearly articulated in the course for the formation of pastoral leaders. This used to be the deacons' year and is now the Graduate Diploma – a collaborative year in which priests, deacons, religious and lay people of all ages study and reflect together. However, this movement in holistic education was already in the College in embryo at a much earlier date.

With the arrival of committees, working parties, and teams, now augmented by part-time lay and religious staff members, structure and process met to form an intricate system of networking, interdependence and shared responsibility.

A professional layman came on board, to help restructure the plant and manage resources in such a way that the vision of All Hallows could be given material expression. Time, energy and resources were carefully husbanded and advice sought, not only from professionals here and abroad, but also from past students who contributed guidance about how the spirit of All Hallows could be captured in the environment. The vision of mission and ministry which motivates those who work here is steeped in tradition and at the same time is flowing with the currents of change.

It was not without risk that a gentle revolution of democratisation took place. There were obstacles and hazards and often times bewilderment. Nevertheless this revolution moved the College from a stance of 'him and us' to 'them and us' and finally to 'us'. It was not a giving away of power but power-sharing, a sharing of power which had energising consequences, and which drew from every level a high degree of commitment.

The 'us' who made up the All Hallows community in the past has changed radically. The staff at all levels – academic, administrative, maintenance – is more inclusive – men and women, lay and clerical, religious and secular. The student body is almost beyond recognition. Gone is the soutane-robed, single sex, same-aged group of young men, and in their place is a multi-faceted complex of inter-relating groups from all social strata – single, married and widowed, lay and religious, young and old, experienced and inexperienced, professionals and neophytes, European and African, American and Asian, Irish and Australian. The dynamic emanating from the interaction of so diverse a group has tremendous potential for a more open education of pastoral ministers.

At the heart of all this change is leadership. The official leaders each have had their own style. The present leader reflects long and carefully before he goes into action. His style is hard to categorise for, like the chameleon, it changes with the environment. The main characteristic is that he facilitates people to own their own power. We are all leaders in one way or another and the focus of leadership shifts from one to another.

I am not sure whether it is the spirit of the house or the quality of the leadership, but something evokes an intense commitment from the people who work here. You get the impression of an anthill – where each one is motivated by a strong sense of purpose – but conscious of the others, carrying the weak, caring for the sad, or keeping the pushy in line.

Change never takes place without pain, and there have been times of confusion, conflict and loss of direction. In terms of learning, it is my experience that the more rooted one is in a mind-set and behaviour patterns, the more resistant one is to change and the greater the suffering.

Coping with change
It is out of that personal experience of observing and being part of a transformation process that I would like to make some observations about ministry today and the process of coping with change.

Among today's concerns, top priority must be given to the universal experience of change. Change is a difficult concept to explain for it is more about experience. It is intrinsic to life and is an on-going process both within the person and outside in society. The problem with change is that it is largely unpredictable and therefore cannot be anticipated. What is new today is the rate of change and the profound effect this has on people and on institutions, particularly on the Church which traditionally changes slowly.

This slow rate of change is not an altogether bad thing. The paradox is that slow change secures stability but it also generates inertia. In terms of ministry in the market place, rapid change requires rapid response and this puts tremendous pressure on both individuals and groups to make on-the-spot decisions. In turn, this creates anxiety and feelings of insecurity and the tendency to run for cover and pretend it is not happening or, conversely, to adopt a rigid pattern of thinking and become defensive and dogmatic. Because of the complexity of modern life, prudence would indicate the need to examine the long term implications of decisions and so tension grows between the pressure for immediacy and the need for good decision making.

Change acts as a stimulant, is exciting and energising, but it also creates uncertainty. In the wake of problems like redundancy, disappearing resources, collapsing family life, increasing lawlessness, growing pollution, the AIDS crisis, the bottom line is that nobody knows what the future holds. In their uncertainty some teachers, for instance, who were happy in their work, see working with travellers as pastorally more immediate. They resign from the structured life of a school and, often completely unprepared, plunge into the unstructured work of relating to the lifestyle of the traveller.

Then there is the search for a course to take the pain out of it and the quest for an answer,'Am I in the right place?' Skills training is often sought as a panacea, but it is never adequate to handle uncertainty. Uncertainty is more to do with perception and attitude than with strategies and techniques. Can the pain and the insecurity be seen as a learning, as a moment of opportunity, or is it written off as failure?

What is certain is that there are trends which can act as guidelines. One of these is the massive change which sends shock waves right through the system, i.e. the shrinking number of people presenting themselves for clerical and religious life. This leaves a smaller ageing group holding on, perplexed and anxious. Uncertainty about the future raises innumerable questions about way of life and ability to cope.

If you spend any length of time in a religious community or among the staff of a seminary, it is easy to pick up the intense anxiety – Who will look after me if I get ill? How am I going to live with all these ageing people? What will happen to me if the numbers drop so low that we have to close down? The faster things change, the faster we have to adapt and the greater the pressure. The rate with which deacons, for instance, have disappeared is phenomenal and the pressure to find new markets from which to attract people to long term commitment is immense. Modern technology increases this sense of acceleration as many of you know from the installation of the answering phone and the fax machine. What the business world calls 'the acceleration syndrome' leaves us in ministry wide open to pressure which results in stress.

Stress has its good side: it keeps us on our toes, focuses the mind. Without it we could be dull and boring. But stress comes from the pressure we or other people put on us to meet deadlines, reach standards, sort out problems. In the kind of work in which we are involved in ministry, there is great emotional drain and often we push ourselves to breaking point. When we pass a certain threshold – then we begin to feel the strain. Stress now costs us not only health but affects our relationships and our ability to make decisions. We communicate poorly, get annoyed quickly and create frustration and confusion everywhere we go. To survive in ministry today we need to be aware of our personal stress threshold and develop powers of adaptation. This has much to do with how we perceive situations, for what to one is a threat, to another is an opportunity. Time spent sitting in a traffic jam can be a threat because of lost time, fear of missing an appointment, letting a group down, or it can be an seen as an opportunity to rest, listen to music, meditate or just think. Our challenge is not to react against change but to respond to it in new ways. To learn to cope with the unexpected and, above all, to discover creative ways of thinking and acting.

Creativity is not the preserve of artists and actors; it is an integral part of the capacity of every person; it is about shifting the iron filings of life and, through the magnetism of our creative energy, giving it a new shape. It is about having a mind which is alert, questioning, receptive, and, above all, rested. It is the antithesis of experiencing a mind which is tired, tense, anxious, depressed or resigned.

In other words stress is the enemy of creativity and the enemy of ministry, for is not ministry about responding sensitively to the nuances of the persons and situations we come in contact with in such a way that we adapt to the uniqueness of each encounter? And yet it is the trap that so many dedicated pastoral persons fall into. A stress reaction most readily happens when we lose sight of the fact that ministry is about keeping the balance between pressure and stimulus.

The key to coping with change and stress-related activities is inner calm. The most pressing need of our time is to develop the capacity to be at peace with ourselves. To find a still centre of inner stability from which we can think and act with clarity. To take time away from our jobs. To be able to dis-identify from our roles, occupations, and preoccupations, to let go and, stripped of our status, be our true selves, is to be able to rest in silence. Inner calm requires a time apart, a meditative presence to myself, and a meditative presence to God. Inner peace makes it possible to meet change with an open mind, to question assumptions fearlessly, to have enough inner flexibility to let go of familiar ways of doing things which no longer serve our purpose, and to risk the unknown. The pull towards activity, getting things done, seeing the fruits of our labour, is intense, but only a time apart will redress the balance. In my experience, this is where pastoral people get trapped. They work till they fall, they lose a sense of perspective, are unable to take time off or to see the opportunities in change. They loose their ability to hang loose. The paradox is that it is the ability to remain calm in the face of change which brings great inner freedom and the flexibility to respond appropriately.

Change in the future – Empowering the laity
I am singling out one area of possible change for the future, that is the empowering of lay people. The great sign of the times is the phenomenal decrease in vocations. There is no indication that this will be reversed in the future. Great expense, in terms of time, energy, personnel and money is laid out on harvesting the remnant. They are coaxed, nurtured and cared for in an unprecedented way. Often their every whim is listened to, discerned and granted. They do, indeed, need to be looked after, but is it not time to move the focus of attention onto people who may shun institutions and long term commitment, but who either have hearts burning within because of an already deep relationship with Jesus, or some vague unspecified ideal which is in the process of being formed? Is it not time to let go of some of our cherished traditions, privileged posi-

tions, sense of achievement and, dare I say, power? Is it not time to pass on our expertise, in whatever area of ministry, to a new group of people? Is it not time to invest money in them, so that they will learn to be in touch with our values, informed with the charisms we cherish, but which now make no impact communicated in the old way and need a fresh voice, and expression in a new language? Is not the hope of the kingdom that a new firm of builders will examine our blueprint, discard what is irrelevant and construct an edifice more in keeping with the needs of the times?

It is very clear that the future will be mainly in the hands of unordained ministers, who must first experience what it means to be a disciple. Maybe the time is right for us to do what Jesus did and issue a personal call to lay people we know to become disciples, to follow him along footpaths already worn by us, but in their own way.

I travel widely in this country and abroad, and the reality is that there is a dearth of religious and clergy everywhere except in the third world. In some countries we are cushioned still against the full impact of the situation, but not so in other parts of the world. My colleague, Joe Walsh, has a parish outside Perth with the quaint name 'Gingin'. It is larger than Ireland and he travels 2,500 km each weekend to say five Masses. Examples such as this could be multiplied. It is also apparent that the average age of professional ministers is alarmingly high, with all the consequences that has for people in leadership roles. How do we prepare them for retirement and who will take their place? There is no doubt that it will be lay people mainly who will bring Christ's face, presence and voice to the people from the year 2,000. Instead of waiting until force of circumstance demands that we appoint a lay person to a post and we go around looking for the right person with the right qualifications, should we not be consciously selecting our successors, forming them, shaping them, evoking from them their unique talents, nurturing in them specifically Christian values and attitudes and fostering their relationship with God?

Is it not time that we exerted pressure to have them adequately remunerated for their services, while at the same time respecting the principle of voluntary service for those who can afford it? Is it not time that the non-ordained minister experienced equality and the sharing of power?

Is it not time that the unique contribution of women be honoured, taken seriously and channelled into the main stream of planning and consultation? It is time that the people who assemble to deliberate and decide represent all the people, for all are made in the image and likeness of God and all are called to God's will. The raising of feminine consciousness is worldwide. Augusta Neal, in an article on the 'Pathology of a Man's Church', says that this revolution, 'Has created a gestalt shift in the whole way of seeing our relations to one another, in such a way that our behaviour patterns are formed from the inside out.' In other words, change of inner attitude is essential. The model that many women are looking for is one of peer relationships and the development of new skills in acting as peers. For me, one of the most fascinating processes to watch in the Graduate Diploma course is the awakening of the men to the pain and sense of oppression women have felt, and the awakening of the women to the powerlessness of many men. Each begin to see the differences in ways of perceiving and articulating experience, and grow in understanding of each other by working as peers on shared projects.

The main contribution of feminine consciousness is a deep sense of relatedness, of being able to see all life as inter-connected and whole. In terms of facilitating ministry, the feminine thrust is instinctively towards building relationships and nurturing them, in such a way as to counteract tendencies towards separateness and competition. Spiritually women are at home with the immanence of God and find his presence easily in ordinary life. What they yearn for is an openness and mutuality through which they can express and share their differences in perception.

Do those who control so many areas of ministry not need to move over and make space for this largely unrepresented section of the community? If we are going to empower lay people in the future, then we must target potential talent.

I often experience frustration when interviewing lay people, apply-
ing for different levels of ministerial formation from part-time lay
ministry programmes to full-time masters programmes. Talented
and eager young men and women present themselves, but lack of
job opportunities or money or both makes them change their mind
and walk away. I would also add that often they are more independent, resourceful and open-minded, than some who do get places
because they have a diocese or a religious order behind them. This
loss of talent is tragic. Is there not some way of finding and employ-
ing the not-so-obvious Christian who is searching for a way to exercise ministry?

At the moment I see two groups to whom we could profitably turn
our attention:

1. The Young and Uncommitted

These young people are exposed to an explosion of information
and a variety of experiences undreamed of by their parents, much
less their grandparents. Yet at an earlier age they are asking for the
meaning of these experiences and are searching for some way of organising and integrating both their creativity and destructiveness.
Some drift from one experience to another with no sense of purpose, wondering who they are, often lonely and lost, greatly in
need of moral parameters. Others are consumed with achieving energy which burns them up and leaves them empty and loveless. At
the level of spirit they are out of touch with the spark of the divine
within, which creates in them an experience of restlessness and a
sense of unfulfilment. It is from this group that I think ministers of
the future may emerge. Our task is to find an approach which will
touch this deep intuitive hunger for God, in whatever language or
image this hunger is expressed.

The challenge to the institutional Church is to create an environment and atmosphere which will facilitate this deep seated desire
for relationship and union with the ground of their being - and to
open up opportunities which would enable them to make a liveli-
hood.

2. The early retired

There is another group which intrigues me and which, from those I have talked to recently, appears to be only waiting for an opening to share its talents and the wisdom of a life-time in the labour market. It consists of the redundant and those who have taken early retirement but who have no desire to be trapped in structures which they see as inflexible. They have a wish to show compassion, share skills, keep close to the sacred, but they are turned off by the offer of Mickey Mouse jobs. They need to be where the action is, in the centre, with responsibilities for decision making in areas which concern them. In mid-life they are experiencing a draw towards interiority, and the complexity of their inner life both intrigues and frightens them.

William Rademacher in his book, *Lay Ministry – A Spiritual and Pastoral Handbook*, suggests that in the hunt for substitutes for dwindling numbers, the Church might well expand the ministries of the baptised and so encourage ordinary people to search for transcendence through lives of service.

I think that the real task for today's pastoral leaders is to listen to the wisdom of their own hearts and to invoke the wisdom of the little people, the marginalised, the poor, the displaced, those trapped in unhappy marriages, those whom wealth and materialism has left lonely and lost.

From this shared wisdom they might evolve a spirituality and structure which will bring meaning and depth to the lives of modern people and give them the opportunity to serve. Perhaps the insight of a medieval Dominican might point the way. I conclude, then, with the words of Eckart:

Spirituality
Is not to be learned
By flight from the world,
By running away from things
Or by turning solitary and going apart from the world.
Rather, we must learn an inner solitude
Wherever, or with whomever we may be
We must learn to penetrate things,
And find God there.

The Rite of Christian Initiation of Adults Twenty Years On

Thomas McHugh

I recall now, with bowed head, a young woman named Anna. We met in 1969, when she expressed a wish to become a Catholic. I approached this task with enthusiasm. 'She will be my first convert,' I thought. For eight months we worked through the New (Dutch) Catechism. When I was satisfied that she was well 'instructed,' she was duly baptised in the presence of the housekeeper, who stood in as godparent at the last minute, and Anna's mother, a west country Methodist. This took place on a quiet Thursday afternoon in an empty church.

Soon after, I read the following notice in the small ads of a Catholic weekly, *The Universe*: 'Convert, recently received, at a loss, would like to meet others in similar circumstances.' This was not Anna, but it might well have been. Clearly I was not the only priest who was failing to give expression to the theological, catechetical and pastoral insights of Vatican II.

In 1972, *The Rite of Christian Initiation of Adults* was promulgated by Rome. It aimed to revive the practice of the early Church of receiving adults through a series of liturgical rites and lengthy catechetical stages: a time of enquiry followed by the rite of entry; a period of catechumenate leading to the rite of election; the Lenten period of 'purification and enlightenment' followed by the celebration of baptism, confirmation and eucharist at the Easter Vigil. My practice with Anna had pointed to a Church that emphasised the institution, in which all ministry was done by the priest; catechesis was about information and credal formulae. In contrast, the rite stresses that welcoming the new Catholic is the responsibility of the whole community. Ministry is shared; conversion is seen as a lifelong journey into the mystery of God revealed in Jesus Christ. Belonging to the Church is seen as discipleship: a sharing in the mission and ministry of Jesus Christ to transform the world and draw all things together in unity.

Yet twenty years later, Aidan Kavanagh warns us that so many bad practices are growing up around the rite that if the present trend continues it will not survive to the year 2,000. It is not a programme, he says, nor is it a process as such. It is a liturgical rite with the same authority and obligations as the *Missa Normativa* of Paul VI.

I, also, fear that the challenge and opportunity offered us by the liturgical rites of Christian initiation of adults are not being fully attended to. All too often, we settle for cosy liturgies which fail to include the wider parish community, limiting involvement only to the candidates, sponsors, catechists, priests and a few friends. Some parishes ignore the rite altogether and adults are received into the Church much as they were twenty years ago. The approach of others to the rite is a modest adaptation of the old 'convert class' that pays little attention to the spirit of the rite as expressed in the introduction to the liturgical texts. No method is neutral. These bad practices deliver their deadly message for the life of the Church.

The challenge in the rite
How the Church goes about initiating new adult members reveals our deepest identity. It provokes the questions: Who are we? What do we stand for? These are recurring questions for any group, which surface especially when an outsider expresses a wish to be part of the group. They are disturbing questions, too, because they are radical. They go to the root of the group's identity and purpose.

From the very beginning, these have been questions for the Church. In the Acts of the Apostles, chapter 11, we are told that Peter was challenged by the Jewish Christians at Jerusalem for welcoming pagans (outsiders) who had accepted the Word of God. He defended himself by telling the story of his own conversion. While at prayer, he had a vision of a big sheet being let down from heaven by its four corners ... and in it were all sorts of wild animals and beasts. He was invited to kill and eat. Peter replied, 'Certainly not,

Lord; nothing profane or unclean has ever passed my lips.' But then the reply came from heaven: 'What God has made clean you have no right to call profane.'(Acts 11:9) Peter had to make his own a new image, whereby Jews and pagans who had heard the Word of God and embraced the vision of Jesus could now be brothers and sisters in one Church, the Body of Christ.

If the first Pope experienced such a conversion in the first century, we too can allow the possibility that we need to face a similar conversion in the twentieth century. Parish communities still face these issues: who is in, who is out? What are the criteria of belonging? What explicit and implicit signals do we give to the interested outsider? Do we recognise that these people may have insights into the truth? Is there room for the outsider at our table? Do they have gifts to bring? How does our Church in its practice compare with that of the Jesus of the gospels?

For several years now, many parishes in the United Kingdom have been welcoming, catechising and celebrating the entry of adults into the Church through The Rite of Christian Initiation of Adults. It is dawning on some that if we take the rites seriously we are faced with challenges at many levels. This is understandable. At stake are issues of identity and purpose. A key question for a parish engaged in the process of initiation will be: What does it mean to be a disciple of Jesus of Nazareth in Britain today? The way we welcome, catechise, celebrate liturgy and engage in ministry in our parishes reveals certain assumptions about what we stand for and what is less significant. It was George Bernard Shaw who said, 'A person's beliefs may be ascertained not so much from his creed but from the assumption upon which he habitually acts.' I repeat, no method is neutral.

It helps to ask the question: What do we think we are doing when we do what we do? To what degree are our thoughts, words, feelings and actions in harmony? I propose in this article to look at four areas of challenge presented by the R.C.I.A.
1. What does it mean to be a Catholic Christian in Britain today?
2. How do we engage in the search for truth?
3. Exploring power in the rite.
4. Who ministers?

What does it mean to be a Catholic Christian in Britain today?

At its best, The Rite of Christian Initiation of Adults offers an opportunity for enquirers, people who are searching for truth and meaning in their lives, to meet with other adults within the Catholic Christian tradition, who are also searching for truth, to explore this question. It is in this context, at this point in history, in this culture, with its sub-cultures, that we encounter truth and falsehood. It is in this setting that we experience the call to be disciples of Jesus of Nazareth, who is the Christ.

We are called to conversion, to God's way of being fully human and fully alive in our time and place in history. This is the way in which we give glory to God (Irenaeus). We are called to participate in the mission and ministry of Jesus, to 'transform the world according to the plan of God in view of the final coming of the kingdom.'[1]

However, the temptation for any parish is to reduce the RCIA to initiating new members into a 'Club' which guarantees personal salvation, a passage to heaven. Much as with the old convert class, we instruct people on our creeds, codes and rituals, answer their questions, even give answers to questions they are not asking. The focus is on Catholic membership rather than conversion and discipleship. This reflects a Church more concerned with maintenance than mission. The following parable makes the point:

On a rocky seacoast there was once a ramshackle life-saving station. It was no more than a hut with one boat, but the few people who worked at the station were devoted. Many lives were saved and the station became famous.

As the fame of the station grew, the people gave time and money. New members were enrolled, boats bought and crews trained. The hut was replaced by a comfortable building and it became a popular gathering place, a local club. As time passed the members became so engaged in socialising that they had little interest in life-saving, though they still wore their badges. In fact, when people were actually rescued, it seemed a nuisance because they were dirty and sick, and soiled the carpets and the furniture.

Soon the social activities of the club became so numerous, and the lifesaving activities so few, that there was a showdown at a club meeting. Some members insisted that they return to their original purpose and activity. After a vote, the troublemakers, a small minority, were invited to leave the club and start another.

This they did, a little further down the coast, with such selflessness and daring that, after a while, their heroism made them famous. Their membership grew, their hut was re-built and their idealism smothered. If you happen to visit that area today, you will find a number of exclusive clubs dotted along the shoreline. Each one of them is justifiably proud of its origin and its tradition. Shipwrecks still occur in those parts, but nobody seems to care much any more. [2]

The great disease of any organisation is amnesia, that is, forgetfulness of origins and purpose as set down by the founder. A parish may become so preoccupied with serving the good of the members that it forgets its primary purpose to proclaim and be the good news of Jesus Christ for others. Every Christian community is called to project the image of Jesus that is faithful to the gospels and to be prophetic in its own time and place. This constitutes the essential mission of every parish and is the 'supreme goal of the Church.' [3]

How do we engage in the search for truth?
Pope Paul VI tells us that the men and women of our generation thirst for authenticity. Young people especially have a horror of the artificial and the false. They are searching above all for truth and honesty. 'Either tacitly or aloud we are being asked: Do you believe what you are preaching? Do you live what you believe? Do you really preach what you live?'[4] These are powerful words from a great pope. They challenge every priest and all who listen to the gospel truth Sunday after Sunday.

These are also the kind of questions we face when adults enquire about becoming a Catholic Christian. Basically, they want to know: How can I be true to my deepest self now, in this place, in this environment? What light do the gospel and Christian tradition throw on it? How do your stories as fellow pilgrims resonate with mine? Is it evident that Christ's Spirit is at work in us, and that we seek to express the values of the gospel in our lives?

Jesus had a fundamental capacity for naming the truth. He spoke with authority because the truth that he spoke openly resonated with what he had come to discover by attending to who and what represented truth and falsehood in the land of Israel in the first century. Because of his unique relationship with his Abba/Father, he himself and even his enemies recognised him to be the agent of God's truth. 'Teacher, we know you are a truthful man and teach God's ways sincerely.'[5]

If the fundamental human call is to choose life, to live in truth with freedom and responsibility, then a key question is, 'What is truth?' Here, the late Cardinal Leger of Montreal is worth quoting: 'Truth,' he said, 'is a mystery to be explored, not something we possess.' This was his response to a document presented to the first post-Vatican II synod by Cardinal Ottavianni which took the form of a 'syllabus of modern errors'. Leger went on to say, 'the draft (document) does not recognise and is not in accord with the spirit of Vatican II.'[6]

Implied in this debate are two approaches to the understanding and communication of truth. I would like now to expand on the implications of these two approaches for catechesis in the RCIA. To use the contemporary language of religious education, Leger's approach to the truth can be termed 'spiral' while Ottavianni's approach is 'linear'.

The linear approach assumes that truth is given from the top down in the Church; that it can be possessed and expressed in neat formulae and transmitted from generation to generation. The linear approach is didactic; it is about handing on packaged truth. The point of arrival is pre-determined before departure. It may offer answers before it hears the questions. Little thought is given to whether it makes a difference to life choices.

Indubitably, many enquirers look for the security of the linear approach. They want 'information about' rather than the kind of knowledge that calls for change and risk. The linear approach makes little or no reference to their life experience. This approach to truth seems to offer stability and certainty but, in fact, controls and restricts. It confirms the hierarchical authority structure and demands conformity to the institution. It focuses on doctrine almost to the exclusion of experience and the possibility of dialogue.

The spiral approach to catechesis, on the other hand, implies the risk of being challenged. It implies openness to people and events, readiness to reflect, share and change. It values people and their story. There is no point at which one can say, 'I have arrived.' It invites questions about where we encounter truth, the real, the living God. The nearer we come to the real, the nearer we come to an encounter with the divine. The spiral approach, then, demands that we be attuned, attentive with our whole being – body, emotions, mind and spirit – to the whole world of human experience, secular and ecclesial, past, present and possible future. This means living life at the boundary of Church and world in dialogue and partnership with others in a common search for the real. This takes us inwards and downwards to our depths (soul) and outwards beyond the boundaries of the ecclesial institution. It requires imagination, readiness to live with questions, openness to the undermining or shattering of our world view, leading to a sort of death in which there is a new 'revelation' for the one who searches.

The spiral approach requires us to bring into dialogue our own story, the story of the inquirers with whom we share the journey, the story of our culture, of the Church and scripture leading into *the* story – God. Clearly, then, the spiral does not preclude doctrine or teaching but rather demands that they be integrated into the search. With rare exceptions, our current practice in catechesis focuses on the Church and its story almost to the total exclusion of the story of the culture. This ensures the continuation of the gap between faith and daily life and the blunting of the prophetic edge of the gospel.

The linear model assumes that the structure and mechanisms of the institutional Church, e.g. hierarchy, sacraments etc, were fixed by

Jesus Christ, while the spiral model assumes a Church emerging, a group of disciples who experienced Jesus of Nazareth in a way that was transformative for them. In the light of the resurrection, they sought to explore the meaning of this experience, and share and celebrate it with others.

The institutional Church may be said to be addicted to the linear model, which is used by the institution to protect and guarantee the control and power of the clergy. The linear is endemic. It is reflected in our liturgies, in our catechetics and our assumptions about ministry, for example: who has the authority to teach? To the linear mindset – which has, to some degree, shaped us all – the spiral is seen as dangerous. The institution under threat from secular pressures and internal demands for change clings to the linear by proposing a catechism for the universal Church.

Those who work with groups of enquirers sometimes ask: Can authentic catechesis be anything other than spiral? Yet we are trapped by the apparent need to ensure that the catechumens have 'got it', i.e. what they need to know to be a Catholic. Furthermore, in the RCIA, we can all too often kid ourselves that we are operating a spiral model if we share (sometimes ignorance) in groups, when, in fact, we may be operating a disguised linear model.

We are reluctant to engage in the spiral model because we want cheap salvation without conversion. We resist inviting others to face true conversion to discipleship because of the demands it would place on us. We avoid the pain of crisis and the cross. The spiral approach is a call to freedom and responsibility. It is a call to respond to and be shaped by a reality greater than ourselves. We settle for 'little destinies' without inviting people into the great destiny. We are afraid of freedom: we prefer to be slaves.

Are we calling people to discipleship, to be partners in mission, at the service of the kingdom, or are we inviting them in the first place to seek security in the Church? The very presence of the enquirer raises the question for us: What does it really mean to be a disciple of Jesus of Nazareth in this time and place?

Our response to this question is the journey of faith. Truth comes to meet us in every moment of our daily experience but we need awareness and discernment. The competence of the disciple is to be attentive to the present reality and to the Word, to participate in the resulting dialectic, to discern and to name the truth and the lies in the present reality of our lives and the world. Then we are called to action by witnessing to our ever-deeper experience of the truth by the choices we make in freedom.

'Jesus did not counsel a passive submission to his word ... but to an active and progressive engagement with it under the influence of the Spirit who will lead us into all truth.'[7] 'If you continue in my word, you are truly my disciple, you will know the truth and the truth will set you free.'[8]

Exploring power in the rite

'No method is neutral.' Nowhere is this more evident than in the celebration of the liturgy, in particular the way we celebrate the initiation of new adult members into our parish communities through The Rite of Christian Initiation of Adults. In the liturgy, words and symbols connect us to the vine and the mystery that is at the depth of each of us.

Through ritual we seek to communicate and to be in communion. We employ words and actions which invite a response. If we use the wrong word or action, we will invariably get the wrong response. This is well illustrated by a story told by Gene Walsh, a writer on matters liturgical in the United States of America:

> Two Arabs were arguing over the price of a camel. After some haggling they agreed on a figure. Salman, the new owner was advised that this camel responded best to certain signals. To get the animal to go into a trot, you used the word 'wow'; and if you wished him to gallop you simply said 'Wow! Wow!' When you wanted the camel to stop, you said 'Amen'.

> Salman, pleased with his new mount, climbed onto it and he said 'Wow!' The camel went into a trot and when Salman cried 'Wow! Wow!' the camel galloped across the desert, leaving clouds of sand in its trail. Salman was exhilarated until, all of a sudden, he saw ahead of him a deep ravine with a sheer drop.

But he had forgotten how to get the animal to stop. In desperation he began to pray aloud to Allah. When he ended the prayer with a great 'Amen', the animal skidded to a halt at the very edge of the precipice. With a great sight of relief, Salman leaned forward over the camel's neck and, on seeing the depth of the ravine, cried 'Wow! Wow!' [9]

A signal once given cannot be recalled. It goes on inexorably to produce its effect. Good signals properly expressed will produce the desired results, and poor signals will have poor results. It can even be said that good liturgy strengthens faith while bad liturgy may undermine faith. All who dare to participate in and celebrate the liturgy must beware of the power placed in their hands! Each of us might well ask what signals do my words, actions, postures in the liturgy convey to those around me? Do they offer life or death to the community?

The liturgical rites are at the heart of the process of initiation of adults. It is in the celebration of the rites that the Christian initiation of adults begins to impinge upon the life of the parish. After all, the liturgy is meant to be the work of the people. Kenneth O'Riordan speaks of the liturgy as coming out of our experience, having that experience confronted by a) the presence of all who have gathered together, b) the Word of God, c) the call to 'do this in memory of me,' d) the call to communion, and e) the call to mission.[10] In this way, it is always a reflection of our reality.

This reality is highlighted repeatedly in the rites. Let me illustrate from the rite of welcome or acceptance into the Order of Catechumens. The unbaptised enquirer stands before the priest, accompanied by his or her sponsor, in the midst of the community. At the beginning of the rite, there is an opening dialogue between the enquirer and the minister which includes this question: What do you ask of God's Church?

This Church is not an abstract reality but something visible, tangible, audible, enfleshed in this community. So, maybe the question could be, What do you seek? What do you ask of this community?

In a real sense, the question is for all who participate: the liturgy is not a spectator sport. The rite offers the answer 'faith', but suggests that the enquirer may wish to express what is in his/her heart using his/her own words. Depending on the answer, the next question in the rite is phrased accordingly. ('What does faith offer you?') Imagine the possibilities and the potential of the whole congregation wrestling with those questions. For we are all seekers together; none of us has yet 'arrived'. Of course, this would demand prior catechesis and careful preparation.

Following the affirmation by the sponsors and the assembly, the candidates are signed with the sign of the cross on the forehead. The cross is the symbol which stands at the heart of the community of disciples. The candidates, at the very beginning of their pilgrimage into the household of faith, are sealed and branded with this sign of contradiction. From now onwards, life is choosing to be a learner and disciple. The meaning of the disciples' life is about giving yourself away, to become who we are called to be, to realise our calling by being with others in community for the life of the world. To what degree have we managed to domesticate the cross, to empty it of its power and meaning in our lives, and divorce it from the real pain and crucifixion in the daily lives of people?

The candidates for baptism are now dismissed in a friendly manner to continue with their sponsors and catechists to break the Word of God. This is a liturgical act which, when done well, cannot fail to evoke questions from the 'cradle Catholics' who remain behind; questions like, 'If they are encouraged to explore the Word and express and share their responses, why not us?' I know of few parishes where the congregation is encouraged to come to Mass ready to share a word on the scripture with those around them before or after the homily.

Many other questions may surface: Why do I come to Mass? Do I believe in the real presence of God in the Word? Why do the candidates go out now that we have just celebrated their entry into the household of the faith? Why do I stay? Do Catholics really believe in sharing the Word of God? Can they do this with or without a priest? If such questions are ignored, an opportunity is missed by the whole Catholic community. Again, we return to the choice between the spiral and linear view of things.

We can opt for the linear with its control from above, people who have arrived delivering the truth to people on the way. Or we can seek to release the power in the rite to transform our lives, and the images deep in our individual and collective psyche which shape our self-understanding, the way we feel, and our behaviour. There is nothing neutral about how we celebrate the rites. Well prepared and celebrated, they renew and deepen the faith life of the community and propel it into mission. On the other hand, even a nice and carefully-prepared liturgy can confirm a people in a holy huddle that has no point or purpose but 'self-serving'.

Who ministers?
A fourth challenge presented by the RCIA is perhaps the greatest, and that is in the area of ministry.

According to the rite the whole community ministers.[11] The initiation of adults is the responsibility of all the baptised. But this is not a question of them and us, whereby the baptised do all the ministering and the enquirers and candidates are the recipients. There is mutuality in ministry. By its nature ministry is relational, for we are all companions on a common pilgrimage who seek meaning, to name the truth and live in it. To acknowledge this requires openness and humility on the part of the Catholic community. The enquirers come with their gifts, their story, their questions and insights into truth. They can become the catalyst for Catholics to hear afresh the call to 'come and see,' to experience the call to conversion. If we are to be effective ministers, we need to stand as it were in the enquirers' and candidates' shoes, learn to use their language, to appreciate the system of symbols that constitute their world of meaning. At some level, the enquirer/catechumen invites the Catholic community to explore with him/her the question: 'What does it mean to be a Catholic Christian in this time, place and culture?' By engaging in the formation of new disciples the whole community is challenged to examine the meaning of discipleship for themselves. The lay persons and clergy alike are invited to look to the prime source of their ministry, the sacraments of initiation: baptism, confirmation and the eucharist.

However, as Catholics, we too easily exist in a cosy Catholic world where the language and symbols are divorced from the world in which we live. 'This split between faith, which many profess, and their lives deserves to be counted among the most serious errors of our age.'[12] We are often so concerned that the enquirer should take on our traditions, rituals, rules and formulae that we do not leave room to explore this one essential question of the meaning of discipleship in our society. We end up placing burdens on their shoulders which enslave rather than liberate. We need to take note of the words of John Paul II in *Christifideles Laici* 59, '... a faith that does not affect a person's culture is a faith not fully embraced, not entirely thought out, not fully lived.'

The enquirers/catechumens minister to the community in that they can help to keep the focus of the Church's ministry on service to the world for the building up of the kingdom. Their ministry can ensure that our catechesis for discipleship remains focused on the kingdom of truth, life, holiness and grace, justice, love and peace.[13] However, we need to recognise that not every enquirer wants to face the gospel demands of discipleship. They may, in fact, be seeking the 'shadow security' of belonging to this nice group of people who do not appear to make too many demands on their life-style or be at odds with the values of society around them.

Ideally, lay people will be challenged to discover that 'their own field of evangelising activity is in the vast and complicated world of politics, society and economics, as well as the world of culture, of science, of the arts, of international life, of the mass media. It also includes other realities which are open to evangelisation, such as human love, the family, the education of children and adolescents, professional work and suffering.'[14]

Catechesis and formation for this understanding of lay ministry, as much as catechesis for the sacraments, should shape the content and process of catechesis during the RCIA.

Once initiated, the new Catholics ... 'enter a closer relationship with the faithful and bring them renewed vision and a new impetus.'[15] This demands an openness to ongoing conversion on the part of the community which needs to discover afresh the meaning of discipleship and the proper locus for its ministry.

Through the rite, therefore, it is possible to recognise the ministry of the enquirer and the catechumen to the Catholic community. Yet the rite also invites challenges to the way that ministry has been traditionally understood within the community. In the RCIA group, the priest, lay people, and enquirers or catechumens explore the same life questions in the light of each other's faith stories, and the story of the culture in the light of the story of Christian tradition. This process, properly understood, cannot help but lead to a change or conversion in the way that group members experience themselves in relation to one another.

The starting point for the group is the validity of each person's lived experience. All are respected as sons and daughters of God. Each comes with his or her particular gift for the good of the whole. The basis of all ministry is our shared life in Christ through the sacraments of initiation. By participating in the life, ministry and mission of Jesus, each according to our own calling and in our given situation, we image Jesus in our time, place and culture. It is by engaging in our Christian ministry that we become who we are called to be, images of Christ.

With this theological basis for ministry, a new form of relationship is demanded between priest and lay people – a shift from the hierarchical model to a model based on 'communio'. Genuine collaboration in ministry between ordained and lay people, including religious, and men and women is necessary for the mission of the Church to be effective. 'The activity of the lay faithful within parishes is so necessary that without it, priests are generally unable to work with full effectiveness.'[16] Nowhere is this more evident in parish life than in preparing for and celebrating The Rite of Christian Initiation of Adults.

Experience shows that this can be at once very threatening and liberating for priests. We were brought up and nurtured in a Church with a strong clerical bias. Authority is vested in and decisions made by male,celibate priests. This has become a way of thinking, feeling and behaving in the Church. Michael Crosby, in The Dysfunctional Church, suggests that most energy in the Church is invested in the maintenance of the institution at the expense of mission and formation of new members for discipleship. 'The maintenance of patriarchal clericalism in Catholicism has supplanted the message and mission of Jesus.'[17] He quotes John Coleman SJ: 'The hierarchical principle in the world of Catholicism is the first and strongest non-negotiable institutional interest of the Church. The Vatican will risk polarising and splitting national innovation, rather than yield power over episcopal appointments.' [18]

In such a Church, lay ministry is by participation in the ministry of the hierarchy. Some priests and lay people, too, will speak of the role of the lay person in the Church as one of 'helping Father'. Yet collaboration in the whole process of initiation of adults into our communities is already beginning to challenge the Church's addiction to the male, celibate, clerically-controlled model of Church and ministry. This gives rise to a tension between two ways of thinking, feeling, behaving in relation to the Church, its ministry and mission. This is true for clergy and lay people alike. Under pressure and at times of greatest vulnerability, the temptation will be to turn to the strongly hierarchical clerical model. Many clergy and lay people succumb.

Collaboration is built on mutual trust and a valuing of each other's worth and equality in dignity and action, based on our shared humanity and life in Christ through the sacraments of baptism, confirmation and eucharist. All share the call to be disciples, co-workers in building the kingdom of God. Collaborators in ministry will value complementarity and be mutually accountable. They will risk openness and vulnerability in the interest of service. They will value what they have in common and know that their differences are for mutual enrichment. They will seek to accept and name their limitations while recognising and affirming each other's gifts and strengths. Those who would collaborate will be as ready to have their feet washed as to wash the feet of another. Collaboration, then, is about a new way of being Church together which, when the RCIA is at its best in a parish, is uniquely expressed in the rich variety and complementarity of ministries.

I would offer one word of caution to all who minister in the initiation of adults into the Christian community; it is on the clericalisation of ministry. There is a real danger that we use the RCIA to reinforce a clerical, celibate, hierarchical model of Church. To guard against this, we need to recognise that all ministry is for service, ultimately the service of the kingdom of God. It is about revealing and sharing the gift of God's presence. Jesus is the Minister of God's presence *par excellence* in and for the world. He comes to minister the saving presence of God to the world. The call of the Christian disciple is to do likewise, to witness to the presence and action of the God of Jesus Christ in our world.

In conclusion, I suggest that the implementation of The Rite of Christian Initiation of Adults is a way of being Church. It helps us to focus on our identity and purpose as Church. It challenges us all, cradle Catholic and would-be-Catholic alike, to conversion at many levels – to recognise that conversion is a lifelong journey into the mystery of God, the source of truth, life, holiness, grace, justice, love and peace. It challenges our understanding of and approach to catechesis, liturgy and ministry in the Church and in the world. I believe that the rite has the potential to enable us at parish level to give full expression to the vision of the Church since Vatican II.

Notes

1   *Christifideles Laici*, 1.

2   Anthony de Melo, *Taking flight*, p84.

3   Pope John Paul II.

4   *Evangelisation in the Modern World* , 76.

5   Matthew 22:16

6   Quoted in the Obituary of Cardinal Leger by Peter Hebblethwaite, *The Independent*, 15 November 1991.

7   S. N. Schneiders, *Beyond Patching*, p 71.

8   John 8:32.

9   E. A. Walsh, *The Theology of Celebration*, p 17.

10   Article by Ken O'Riordan, *Liturgy*, 16 No 4.

11   *Rite of Christian Initiation of Adults*, 4.

12   *Gaudium et Spes*, 43.

13   Preface to the Feast of Christ the King.

14   *Christifideles Laici*, 23.

15   *Rite of Christian Initiation of Adults*, 234.

16   *Christifideles Laici*, 27.

17   Michael Crosby, *The Dysfunctional Church*, p 81.

18   *Ibid* p 80.

PART III

A Future for the Ordained Ministry

Person, Face, Presence, Voice
A Context for Ordained Ministry

Thomas Lane

In recent years, there has been much deepening of our understanding of the Christian call in baptism. Much has also been written on all aspects of ordained ministry. While the two callings should be seen as complementing one another, there is always the possibility of a see-saw situation – as one goes up in importance, the other goes down. In the pages that follow, my hope is that reflecting on some recent understandings of ordained ministry will throw light on the unity of all Christian vocations and ministry. My concentration will be on ordination to priesthood; the link points between this and diaconate and episcopate should be obvious enough.

If there is one key to the teaching of the Second Vatican Council on the role of the ordained priest, it is the insisting that priests act 'in the person of Christ'. The fullest expression of the teaching is in the *Decree on the Ministry and Life of Priests*, where it is closely linked with anointing, character and headship: 'priests by the anointing of the Holy Spirit are signed with a special character and so are configured to Christ the priest in such a way that they are able to act in the person of Christ the head.'(Par 2) In all, the expression 'in the person of Christ,' or its equivalent, occurs five times in the *Constitution on the Church*, three times in *The Decree on the Ministry and Life of Priests*, and once in the *Constitution on the Liturgy*. Since the Council, the expression has had a continual, indeed a growing prominence in official Church pronouncements. Pope Paul VI used it often. It has an important place in the *General Instruction on the Roman Missal* (1970), and in the Apostolic Exhortation following on the 1971 Synod. It is given a key importance in the 1976 *Declaration on the Question of the Admission of Women to the Ministerial Priesthood*. Among

the many contexts in which Pope John Paul II has used it is in articulating the dignity of women and the role of the lay faithful. The
Congregation for the Doctrine of the Faith has been using it quite a
lot since 1973. The new Code of Canon Law uses the expression
three times, notably in the nearest it comes to a definition of the
Sacrament of Orders:899, 2; 900,1; 1008. It features in Pope John
Paul II's *Apostolic Exhortation on the Formation of Priests*, 1992. In
summary, it can be said that the fathers of the Second Vatican
Council used the expression 'in the person of Christ' consciously
and exclusively to describe the place of the baptised who are called
to ordained ministry; this, in turn, has led to its further use to illu-
mine such topics as the relationship between ordained and non-
ordained ministry, the 'essential difference' between baptismal
priesthood and ordained priesthood, and the ministry of women in
the Church.

Recently, some searching questions have come to be asked about
the origin, meaning and history of the expression.[1] What is fairly
clear is that for the past few decades it has been enjoying a prominence and an importance which was never before afforded it. More
controversially, one could ask whether it has come to be loaded
with more meaning than it can easily carry, meaning that might be
re-distributed among some other doctrinal expressions. What is
significant is that the bishops at the Council saw no great need to
explore the expression from the point of view of exegesis and history; they saw it as putting well what they wanted to say about ordained ministry now, and they were satisfied that the phrase and
its near equivalents were to be found in many important Church
sources, including some patristic writings. Recent study of the
expression has shown some interesting developments over the centuries.[2] In patristic writing generally, the Church rather than the
ordained minister was seen as acting 'in the person of Christ'. The
shift of emphasis seems to have come with Aquinas. His use of the
expressions 'in the person of Christ' and 'in the person of the
Church' is highly nuanced.[3] In the celebration of the eucharist, he
saw the priest as acting 'in the person of Christ' because it is here

that Christ acts in a unique way through him. Similar use of the expression in describing the role of the priest is found in such writers as Albert the Great, Scotus, Bellarmine, and Suarez. The Council of Florence took up the teaching: the priest speaks in the person of Christ in effecting the eucharist. The Council of Trent does not use the expression. It was used by Cardinal de Berulle who so much influenced the French school of spirituality. A phrase like 'in the person of Christ' was used by Pope Pius XI in his encyclical on Catholic Priesthood. In *Mediator Dei*, Pope Pius XII made strong connections between the person of Jesus Christ and the person of the priestly minister.

In all the searching into the history of the phrase 'in the person of Christ,' nobody has denied that it comes originally from 2 Corinthians 2:10. The context there is a delicate pastoral work of reconciliation in which Paul was involved. After a longish appeal to the Corinthian community for the forgiving of an unnamed offender, he states that he himself was forgiving him, for the community's sake, in the *persona* of Christ. In these days, in which the exact meaning of the expression is being explored, it is interesting that translators do not opt for 'in the person of'. Versions include 'in the presence,' 'before,' 'in the sight of' Christ; 'by Christ's authority'; 'as the representative of' Christ.

More significant again is the searching question: Is it true that only the ordained person acts in the person of Christ? Could the words not be properly applied to all the baptised, especially in the situations in which they are ministers of sacraments? There is an analogy here with the expression 'other Christs.' For long, this was applied only to people in ordained ministry; the more the riches of the baptismal call have been explored, the more it has come to be applied to all the baptised. Questions have given rise to other questions. Why does St Paul, who elsewhere has very apt words to express presence, choose to use a less familiar word to express the decision he had made with Christ's authority? Why did St Jerome choose to translate Paul by the words 'in the person of Christ'? Was it because the word *persona* was already showing signs of developing a very high profile in western theological discussion, a profile that was to reach one great highpoint at the Council of Chalcedon (451), and that got many further refinements according as the Word of God, in hypostatic union with a human nature, came to be seen as the one subject of divine-human actions?; a profile that led Aquinas to say that a person means that which is most perfect in nature. And we know that, as the shaping of this profile gained momentum, the word person was gaining an ever richer sacramental connotation, a richness which is still unfolding in a Church which now sees herself as the 'universal sacrament of salvation.'[4] In the light of this unfolding, are we likely to see some further developments in the application of the phrase 'in the person of Christ' to ordained ministry? Is there a possibility that it might somehow come to be applied to other members of the baptised?

The questions are complex and each affects the others. As we approach them, it is helpful to look closely at the words St Paul actually used. He had forgiven in the *prosopon* of Christ, literally before/in front of/on the side of/in the presence of, the *face*, the *countenance*, the *eye* of Christ.[5] *Prosopon* was the word for the human face.[6] In Greek drama, especially religious drama, the *prosopon* was the actor's mask. The Latin *persona* had basically the same meaning. It had the extra nuance of emphasising the place of the voice, the sound that came through the mask. The one being portrayed 'sounded through', spoke through, 'sonated' and 'personated' through the mask. This seems to be the most accepted explanation of the origin of the word 'person'. In passing, it is worth noting that, though we associate the use of masks largely with bygone cultures, their proper use was, and still is, a very powerful medium of communication.

The Greek word draws attention to the face. The Latin word emphasises the voice coming through the mask. Both help us to appreciate the fact that an actor was regarded as good to the extent to which he was true to and, in a very real sense, became the one he portrayed and represented, and thus made present the one portrayed.[7] Add to this basic meaning the high profile which the word person has developed, and there is no surprise that the bishops at Vatican II found it an ideal focal point for where they saw that the theology of ordained priesthood had reached, and what they wanted to say and teach about it. They knew that there had been a number of stages in the development of ordained priesthood, notably:

* The calling, formation and commissioning of the Apostles;

* The emergence of fellow-workers of the Apostles whose task is expressed, for example, in St Paul's speaking of 'Fellow-workers'(1 Cor 3:9); 'Stewards of mysteries'(1 Cor 4:1); 'Envoys' (2 Cor 2:7); 'Ambassadors'(2 Cor 5:10); 'entrusted with the Ministry of Reconciliation'(2 Cor 5:18-19);

* The development of the Church's understanding of the sacrificial nature of the eucharist and the importance of suitable provision for its presidency;

* The clarifying of the role of bishop and presbyter in this;

* The shaping of ordination rites for bishops, priests and deacons;

* The contributions of councils, popes, theological and devotional writing.

With this background, their decision to apply the expression 'in the person of Christ' to no other sacrament but orders was a very deliberate one, and still one can now say that, as we set ourselves a different task and explore again the ingredients of the expression, we will find it a very fruitful source for points of contact between ordained and non-ordained ministry. Church teaching is insistent on the 'essential difference' between the two, but this difference must not give the impression of an iron wall of separation. The meeting points are far more important than the differences, since the two are 'by their very nature related to one another'(LG 10) and together they manifest the one priesthood of our one high-priest; the candles of both are lit from the one paschal candle and, in turn, they help to light each other. A continual exploring of the *persona* expression can throw light on how they are related. In fact, as we see the many ways in which baptismal priesthood and ordained priesthood intersect, the clearer we can see what is distinctive about each. Every ministry in the name of Jesus Christ and of his Church is a manifestation of the face, the presence, the voice of God. This is particularly apt at a time of universal yearning for all

that is authentically personal and what promotes the inter-
personal. Our Christian religion is proud to be a religion of persons,
divine and human, and proud that it is ever seeking to unfold the
riches of the incarnation, in which a divine person identified in a
unique way with our humanness. Is it any wonder that as spirituality today draws on the resources of psychology, we are more aware
than before of the many personas which we all wear and the implications of our many masks?

The face

The face reveals the person. In a sense, the face is the person. It
speaks the whole range of our thoughts, our feelings, our affect-
ions. Every language has its 'face vocabulary': we save face, we lose
face, we show face, we face issues. The bible has severe things to
say about those who made graven images. The basic reason was
that the creator's face is beyond depicting. And still there was a
tension. Though no one ever saw God(Jn 1:18), we are assured that
the Lord used to speak to Moses face to face, as one 'speaks to a
friend.'(Ex 33:11) Whatever the exact nature of the experience of the
first Moses, it was in the face of the second Moses, at whose trans-
figuration Moses and Elijah appeared, that the glory of God was
finally and uniquely manifested. His disciples watched his face
light up while he prayed to his Father. It must have been the same
attraction of the same face that drew people to discipleship and
that touched hearts with compunction. From the eyes of that face
came the tears which disclosed the Lord's heartbreak and his compassion. We might ask is it any wonder that the stories of the
'Shroud of Turin' and of the 'Towel of Veronica' have had such a
haunting fascination; there was far more involved in these than the
search for two pieces of cloth.

There have been many attempts to express the final destination of
the human race. None has been more successful than 'beatific
vision' – the seeing that will make us fully blessed and that is the
final blossoming of all the ways that God has 'blessed' us, before
and in creation, in the movement started by the call of Abraham
who was assured that he would be a blessing, in the charter of

blessedness in the beatitudes which are about 'seeing God,' and in the anticipation of the final 'Come you that are blessed by my Father.'(Mt 25:34) The assurance of God is that the crown of all his blessing will be seeing him 'as he is.'(1 Jn 3:2), 'face to face'(1 Cor 13:12). The purpose of all pastoral ministry is to enable people to have 'beatific vision,' even in this life, to help them 'count their blessings' and see how God is blessing them in every event in life and in death and beyond; to keep their eyes 'fixed on Jesus'(Heb 12:2); to make their faces 'light up,' even when all odds seem stacked against them. In the same spirit, all pastoral ministry is a work of removing: helping to remove from people whatever is closing their eyes to the vision that is beatific, since we all tend to see in a sin-damaged way. This opening of the eyes requires a continual range of conversions if we are to keep seeing people and events not with the 'eyes of the foolish'(Wis 3:2) but 'with far-seeing eyes' (Num 24:3).

All those called by God in Christ are invited to mirror to the world something of the infinite riches of the face of God. A man who has an eye and a heart for the beautiful recently spent a whole day entranced before an El Greco painting of St Francis in ecstasy. This was the effect on unaided human eyes of a painting of a human face by human hands; it gives us some glimpse of the riches of the real face of God, fully disclosed. The face of God incarnate uniquely disclosed that real face. The face of his mother disclosed it in a way that only a woman could. One would hope that it is this yearning to experience the feminine face of God that is behind much of the search for the feminine in Church ministry today. A man manifests the riches of God in one way, a woman in another way; each man, each woman, made, as they are, each one in the image and likeness of God, in their own way; the religious, faithful to the charism of his or her community, reflects it in one way, the lay person in another way; the ordained one way, the non-ordained another. At a time of some concern about Church numbers, we can take heart from the fact that one face can light up a whole universe. One has only to think of Pope John XXIII, Pope John Paul I, Mother Teresa of Calcutta.

The author who thirty years ago wrote *Honest to God*,[8] later wrote a less controversial book on the implications of the incarnation, and entitled it *The Human Face of God*. It led to many more books on the face of God and the face of the Church. Recently we have had such titles as *The Human Face of the Church, The Maternal Face of God, Touching the Face of God, Feminine Face of the People of God*. The titles suggest more than a passing fashion. They keep underlining what people yearn to receive from the Church and her ministers: 'Your face, Lord, do I seek. Do not hide your face from me'(Ps 27:8-9). Every generation voices its protests against what it perceives to be faceless people and faceless systems. Invariably we get a new hope when we find any leader in whom we recognise a face that is true in the way that the God of the Covenant is true. We get a new conviction that God is still gracious, that he is still blessing us, that his face is still shedding its light upon us.(Ps 67:1)

The presence

There is a close connection between the 'face' of God and the 'presence' of God, between the face of Jesus Christ and the presence of Jesus Christ. There are good grounds for saying that the most far-reaching teaching of the Second Vatican Council is what it had to say about the related topics of:
1) the presence of Christ in his Church;
2) the presence and action of his grace in every man and woman of goodwill;
3) the fact that belief in the kingdom of Christ should spur us on to develop this earth in the expectancy of a new earth – this earth which is already being enriched by his risen presence.(*GS* par 39)

1) *The Constitution on the Liturgy* (par 7) taught that 'Christ is always present in his Church, especially in her liturgical celebrations. He is present in the sacrifice of the Mass ... in the person of the minister ... in the eucharistic species ... He is present in the sacraments ... in his Word ... When the Church prays and sings ...' This realness of the presence of Christ has been re-affirmed in the *General Instruction on the Roman Missal* (chap 2, par 7) and elsewhere. It has, in turn,

helped us to see Christ himself as the 'primordial' sacrament of God's presence in the world, and to see the Church as the basic sacrament of Christ's presence. It has enriched our whole understanding of the words 'real presence,' as we look at the real presence of the Word in the humanness of Jesus, in a union that is 'hypostatic,' i.e. 'centred on a person,' as the basis of his other presences. All this provides a fine context for our approach to that special refining of real presence which we recognise in the eucharistic celebration and the eucharistic species. It also suggests new ways of imaging his real presence in the peace which he left us and gives us (Jn 14:27), in the mission he gives us (Lk 10:26), in the power he gives us to do greater things than he did (Jn 14:12), in his suffering members (Mt 25:42; Acts 9:4), in the communications he provides us with him and his Father (Jn 14:20).

2) Closely related to the Council's teaching that the Lord is always present to his Church is the teaching on the action of his grace in all men and women of goodwill, not just those with a recognisable Church affiliation. A foundation text here is in *LG*, par 16: 'Those who, through no fault of their own, do not know the gospel of Christ or his Church, but who nevertheless seek God with a sincere heart and moved by grace ... Nor shall Divine Providence deny the assistance necessary for salvation to those who ... have not yet arrived at an explicit knowledge of God, and who, not without grace, strive to lead a good life.'

The implications of this teaching are far-reaching. It has been providing a rich foundation for inter-faith dialogue, and it has had a prominent place in the teaching of Pope John Paul II, notably in his encyclicals on redemption, divine mercy, and mission.

3) The teaching on the presence of Christ and on the face of Christ is inseparable from the Council's teaching on the Lord as the Alpha and Omega, 'The Goal of Human History, the Focal Point of the Desires of History and Civilisation, the Centre of Mankind, the Joy of all Hearts and the fulfilment of all aspirations'(*GS* par 45). This, in turn, links closely with the teaching on the relationship between this earth and the new earth to which we look forward. The pres-

ence, the grace and the transforming action of the Risen Christ help us to see the whole universe as one house, the whole human family as one household, with the Lord himself as the householder, an image provided by more than one gospel parable (e.g. Lk 14:21). [9]

As we look at the ways that the Risen Lord is always present in his Church, at the workings of his grace in all hearts of goodwill, at the fact that he is the focal point of the desires of history and civilisation, we can say that there are many real presences of Christ in the world. In another sense, we can say that there are many manifestations of his one real presence, for 'in him all things hold together' (Col 1:17). The mission of all those who minister in the name of Christ is to be alert to, and to alert others to, the whole range of the manifestations of the presence of Christ in each person's life and in each event that has a bearing on that life. It must aim at helping each person to see how Christ's real presence is compatible with his 'absence,' since only heaven can properly 'keep' him 'till the universal restoration comes' (Acts 3:21). The ideal for everybody in Christian ministry is to be fully present to each person in the whole range of their experiences, especially in the ones that appear to be absurd and senseless; to help each person to be 'really present' to him/herself, his/her neighbour, to Christ, to the Father; in all human seasons, especially when a human heart tends to cry: 'How like a Winter has my absence been, from thee ...' [10]

One hopes that an effect of the acute and distressing shortage of people in some forms of Church ministry, which we are experiencing now and which shows no signs of abating, will have one good effect: to try to find new ways of re-discovering and celebrating the many forgotten forms of the presence of Christ, and to find ways of living with his 'absences'.

The voice

Through the *persona* comes the voice. The one who speaks 'personates' (L. *sonare*, to sound) through the mask. The Christian application is simple. God speaks through people and through events involving people. He has spoken many words, notably in the creation of the world and in introducing the new creation: 'Long ago God spoke to our ancestors in many and various ways ... in these last days he has spoken to us by a Son' (Heb 1:1-2). In the psalmist's vision 'Day to day pours forth speech ... their voice goes out through all the earth, and their words to the end of the world'(Ps 19:2-4). All God's ways of speaking are summed up in the Word who was from the beginning and who became flesh and lived among us (Jn 1:14), and caused amazement by the gracious words that came from his mouth (Lk 4:22). With this background, the task of all ministry is to bring the living Word of God into every area of people's lives and to allow it to 'become flesh'. From the beginning, this has been the great thrust of the proclamation of the gospel. The voice that went out to all the earth (Rom 10:18) became the living word of the apostles. As far as God is concerned, his word never returns to him empty (Is 55:11). In our age when people listen more willingly to witnesses rather than to teachers and listen to teachers only because they are witnesses (*EN* par 41), the Church of the Word made flesh must make sure that it does not become a wordy Church. It must learn to keep 'resonating' with the heart and voice of Christ. And in these days of 'preferential options', especially for the poor, all those in Church ministry should be providing a voice for those who have no voice. There is a very real sense in which power today is in voice.

The ordained priest
A man is ordained to be a face, a presence, a voice, in the name of Jesus Christ who is:
* The shepherd who reveals the Father's merciful and faithful face, and knows his own and is known by them (Jn 10:14);
* The priest who by his perfect sacrifice has gained entry to the presence of God in the heavenly holy of holies (Heb 9:24);
* The prophet who heard the Father's voice and spoke only what he heard from his Father.

The ordained person can never afford to forget that he has no monopoly of sharing in this triple mission of Christ. The Body of Christ on earth is the whole community of the baptised. It is to this whole body, this whole community, that Christ has passed on his mission in the form of shepherding, priesthood, and prophesy. The whole of the baptised people is called to be a ministering people. But in a Church which has one Lord, one faith, one baptism (Eph 4:5) and which must keep moving towards the ideal 'that they may all be one'(Jn 17:21), ordination provides a sacrament of one-ness. All Christian ministry, pastoral, priestly and prophetic, exists to reflect the face of God and in that sense must be exercised 'face to face' with people and with God. This is true of the eucharist, of the celebration of every sacrament, and indeed of every pastoral ministry. The ordained priest brings all these 'facings' into one focus, especially when the Church is most characteristically herself, in the celebration of the eucharist. As a sacramental person, he becomes a face for the myriad faces of people, bringing into focus the members of the many-membered sacrament of salvation which comprise the baptised as 'sacrament' of the saving Christ. Jesus in his lifetime did not answer the very important question, 'By what authority?' He let the answer unfold in his deeds and in the handing on of apostolic office which was to be an integral part of his many-gifted Church. By ordination, the Church, in turn, through her already authorised leaders, assures her members that she is authorising and empowering the person being ordained, for the building up of the whole Church. This authorising and empowering is done by the sacramental word, by the imposition of hands, by anointing and by the conferring of the 'character' of ordination (cf PO par 2). When this character, this sealing, is seen not as a personal gift for the ordained but as a special gift for the further enriching of the whole community of those sealed in baptism and confirmation, the priesthood of the ordained and the priesthood of all the baptised blend harmoniously with the priesthood of our one high priest. The gift of ordination helps to disclose, make blossom, and unite the gifts of all the baptised. To continue the image of personating, the voices of praise from priest, people and the interceding Christ (cf Heb 7:25) together shape a 'sonata' of praise that glorifies God. The ordained priest is the 'guarantor' for the community of the baptised that each eucharistic celebration is a true 'appearing' of the Risen Lord who has 'entered into heaven itself, now to appear in the presence of God on our behalf'(Heb 9:24). This is the significance of the fact that, in the list of the ways in which Christ is present in liturgical celebrations, a special presence is linked with the person of the minister. This presence is for the gathering and lifting up of the gifts of all the members of the body.

There have been many attempts to answer the question, 'What is the theological starting-point for a definition of the priestly ministry?' I remain convinced that the most satisfying answer has been provided by Karl Rahner:[11] 'The priest ... preaches the Word of God by mandate of the Church ... in such a way that he is entrusted with the highest levels of sacramental intensity of this Word ...' In the same context, Rahner emphasises that 'the proclaiming of the Word and the administering of the sacraments have ... a common root and are ultimately one in nature.' The sacramental word is spoken jointly by the Word of God and by the special minister of the Word.[12] When the Word of God is proclaimed at its highest level of sacramental intensity, especially in the sacraments of eucharist and reconciliation, the priest exercises a unique sharing of Christ's headship of the Church. In the eucharist, he is presiding at the celebration which is the summit and source of the whole Church's existence (SC par 10). In the sacrament of reconciliation, he is speaking words which are the high sacramental point of a process that should be going on all the time in all the Christian community. In both, the headship of the ordained person is the sacramental assurance of the saving presence of Christ to all the members of his body. This is why the fuller description of priesthood in the teaching of the Second Vatican Council is in terms of acting in the person of Christ 'the Head'. And this headship is not confined to sacramental activity. It overflows into every expression of pastoral care, which, at its best, is seen as bringing the Word of God into every human situation. Pastoral caring is a function of the Word. The preached word, the Word proclaimed in sacrament, and the pastoral Word are one.

In the continual cycle of ministries in which Word leads up to sacrament and out to pastoral care and back again to sacrament, the priest must be truly a man of face, a face that reflects the heart and voice of the Good Shepherd. It is in line with this vision that the Second Vatican Council presented celibacy as at once a sign of pas-

toral charity and an incentive to it (*PO* par 16). In the man of true
pastoral charity, Word, sacrament and pastoral care converge and
authenticate each other.[13] Sunday celebration will be unreal without weekday pastoral concern; the real meaning and purpose of
pastoral concern will be unfolded on Sunday. All this will show in
the face of one who is always strongly present to the Christian community, and who is not just one who puts in appearances. True to
the mystery of the incarnation, his ministry will always be 'embodied' in day to day realities of the lives of people. His concerns will
be 'spiritual' but not in a way that denies the body; rather, they will
be characterised by the 'glow' of God's Spirit. He will encourage
the development of human talent wherever he recognises it and especially in all those with whom he shares pastoral ministry and
who, in turn, affirm his own giftedness. He will be alert to the findings of any research that throws light on the unity of body, mind
and spirit. The best ways of doing this must be discerned in each
new situation, each new generation. The details as to how ministerial priesthood is to relate to and overflow into and intersect with
'secular', 'political', 'social' and 'educational' activity will vary in
different human situations.

Does the ordained priest directly represent Christ, or does he
directly represent the priestly people, and through them represent
Christ, the Head of the Body, thus acting 'in the person of the
Church'?[14] From the perspective of Christ's handing over his
whole mission to his whole body, the second approach seems to be
the more satisfying one. The priest's ministry finds its meaning
only in the heart of the people whose faith and communion he represents. The priest's unique way of imaging Christ is by representing Christ the head to the members of the living body, all of whom
themselves represent and image Christ in unique and irreplaceable
ways. He is to be a representative of the community of represent-
ers. Representing is a key word here. As well as being prominent in
Catholic thought, it has an important place in the ARCIC and Lima
ecumenical statements. The priest represents Christ who is the
head of the body to whom he has handed over his mission. This representing means that he is an effective sign of the continual active

presence of the head to the members of the body. He is a sacramental representation of the person of Christ, 'a sacramental person at the heart of the sacrament Church'.[15] There are times, even in
the eucharist, when his words are in the form of reported speech. In
addressing the Father about the work accomplished by his Son, he
speaks of the Son in the third person: 'He took bread ... he blessed
...' But what is special to his sacramental role is that he speaks in
the person of Christ, the head of the body of the faithful. He is both
related to the head through the Church and through the head to the
Church. Over seven centuries ago, Aquinas described ordained
priesthood in terms of instrumental causality. In these days of the
primacy of persons, the language of instruments may seem strange
and arid. But, significantly, talk of human instruments is getting a
new prominence in Christian writing. And nobody has written
more sensitively about human instruments than did Aquinas. In
the eucharist especially, he saw the whole priestly people as raised
to a special level of instrumentality. In this setting, he pointed out
the necessity that there be only one minister who represents
Christ.[16] His understanding of instrumentality is closely linked
with his understanding of sacramental character and its place in
the special participation of the ordained person in the priesthood of
Christ.

With the concern today for the promoting of the role of the lay
faithful, and with the desire for the revealing of the feminine
aspects of the face of God, does the emphasis on the specialness of
ordained ministry inevitably downgrade all other forms of ministry? It would be easy to be dismissive of the profound and anguish-
ing problems which this question continues to raise. The question
must be continually put in the right perspective. The ordained person acts in the person of Christ, the head. In the imagery of St Paul
the head expresses authority, but, at the same time and insepara-
bly, it expresses the giving of life and the encouraging of life. The
headship of Christ is never a headship of domination or mastery
since Christian power is the exact opposite of worldly power. The
only headship which Christ recognises as exercised in his name is a
headship of love, a headship of self-giving, a headship of self-

sacrifice, a headship of service, a headship in which the head is in continual life-giving organic interaction with all the members of the body, all of whom share his kingly, priestly and prophetic mission. It is the headship of the one who 'loved the Church and gave himself up for her ... That she may be holy and without blemish' (Eph 5:25-27). It is the headship of the one who taught '... with you this must not happen. No, the greatest among you must behave as if he were the youngest, the leader as if he were the one who serves ...' (Lk 22:24-27). The Christ who is described in Church statements about the question of the admission of women to priesthood is the bridegroom who loved his Church and gave himself up for her. And the unbroken tradition of the Church, on which these statements see themselves based, is claimed to be a mirroring of the continual faithfulness of Christ to his bride, a faithfulness which in turn unfolds the nuptial relationship between his Father and his people. The nuptial symbol describing the union of Christ with his bride, the Church, has at least strong moral implications, in terms of fidelity, and devotion, for the place of ministry in the Church at all times.[17] It is interesting that the nuptial meaning of the body has had a prominent place in the thinking and teaching of Pope John Paul II. In his teaching on marriage, the equality of the partners is getting a growing prominence. In his unravelling of the meaning of the husband/wife relationship in Ephesians 5, in his letter on the *Dignity of Women*, he is at pains to separate the new elements brought by Christ from the old elements inherited from Judaism. He concludes that the 'subjection' called for by St Paul is not the subjection of one partner to another but the mutual self-donation of both. As the implications of this teaching come to be absorbed into our understanding of Church ministry, one can hope for an ever richer expression of the mutuality of all services to the body. This mutuality cannot be expressed in the context of rights, power, cultural conditioning, superiority/inferiority. Its only authentic expression will be by going back to Christ's sacrificial love for his Church, a love which must pervade all ministry exercised in his name. Ordained ministry must continue to express this love sacramentally. It must keep renewing itself in the mystery of the incarnation and in the once-for-all sacrifice (Heb 9:12) of our one priest.

Any day on which ministerial priesthood is perceived as domination or monopoly is a day on which what should be light has been turned into darkness. It is for the same reason that the ordained person should see no threat in sharing many of the elements of 'in the person of Christ' with the rest of the baptised. The fact that, in official Church usage, the expression is applied only to the ordained is a continual reminder of that 'headship' and unique relationship to the Word that is proper to the ordained.

Does the language of 'in the person of Christ' suggest acting a part and impersonation? As always, we are dealing here with the limitations of all human language and imagery. There certainly is an ambivalence in the mask image, in particular. The man who wears a mask or persona can become a caricature or a phantom person. A persona can conceal and distort, as well as reveal. The suggestion of 'masked men' can have hideous connotations. The hardest thing Jesus said about the Pharisees was that they were 'hypocrites', literally stage-actors. But being 'in persona' is a programme and a lifelong process. All through his life, the ordained person is invited to grow into the persona of Christ, grow up into the head. Instead of seeing him as 'impersonating' Christ, perhaps we should say that he is called to a daily conversion that will enable him to be an authentic image, 'in-personating' Christ.

Spirituality
If pastoral ministry is about face, presence, voice, then the spirituality for the man or woman in ministry must be a search for a face-to-face relationship with God and people, a search for a more real presence on all the levels of one's being, a search for a daily hearing and communicating the voice of the Lord.

If the ordained priest's special role is to proclaim the Word of God at its highest level of sacramental intensity, then in his living out the holiness to which he is called as a member of the baptised, the special characteristic of his spirituality must be *verbo vivere*, to live by the Word. The task of ordained ministry is the continual making of connections, especially between the Word of God and the daily lives of people, and, in turn, between Word and sacrament. This must be done in continual communion with all those who exercise baptismal ministry. The universe had its origins 'from harmony, from heav'nly harmony.'[18] The dream of God for the universe is a world in harmony, in tune. But the world fell out of harmony, in the mess we have come to call original sin. Into a world out of harmony and out of tune, the Son of God came, saying 'I am coming ... to do your will, O God' (Heb 10:7). The letter to the Hebrews gives us the programme of God's own Son for the only true priesthood, the only true sacrifice, the only true at-one-ment:

* He walked every step of life's journey in a way that fully pleased God;
* For us, he has broken through every barrier that separates us from God, and made living contact with every level of human existence, and has led us in the journey into the innermost recesses of the mystery of the living God;
* His sacrifice consisted in pleasing God in every level of his own body, and by giving us all the life-blood that flows from that body;
* He has shown us the way and repaired every stage of the way, to God;
* He has brought to completion all the partial and piecemeal ways that lead to God;
* With our eyes fixed on him, and continually inserted into his one sacrifice, we can in our own bodies offer a sacrifice of praise by our lips, our hearts, and our active hands.
* Obeying our 'leaders' and right participation in the assemblies will help keep us in tune with the one sacrifice of the one priest.

(The Letter to the Hebrews did not develop a doctrine of the sacrificial nature of the Christian eucharist. Neither did it develop a doctrine on what we now call ministerial priesthood. It provided foundations for these developments - much of which took place in the early Christian centuries. The process has been continuing ever since.)

The task of all those who share in the priesthood of the one high priest is to keep re-making the broken connections between earth and heaven where our high priest is. The one who is to proclaim the Word at its highest level of sacramental intensity is in a unique position to keep searching for ways to make the connections. It is encouraging to find that the work of reconciliation in which St Paul was involved, and which provided the context for his expression 'in the person of Christ', required the making of a number of delicate connections, involving him, the offender, the people, and Christ himself (2 Cor 2:5-10).

At a time when the sacrament of reconciliation is taking on a new face, the ordained person must, in communion with all others who exercise ministry, be alert to the needs for reconciliation at various levels of the local community and seek for suitable sacramental connections. The details of these connections differ in the 'old' Christian world, in the newly freed world, in the world emerging from paganism. In all of them there seems to be something of an 'exilic' situation; Christians generally are finding that they cannot easily draw on the reserves of an inherited spiritual patrimony. In an age of spiritual amnesia, people in pastoral ministry are finding themselves in the position that they themselves have to be the Christian memory. With the inroads of many new forms of secularisation, it would seem that we are involved in a Copernican revolution in the work, life-style and prayer-style of those in ordained ministry and in the re-shaping of their relationships with men and women in full-time or part-time Church ministry.

There is much to be said for the claim that 'the devout Christian of the future will be either a mystic ... or he will cease to be anything at all.'[19] Ordination is a call to be a 'mystic' and an encourager of those willing to live and be immersed in the mystery of Christ and his Church. In the future, more than ever, this will demand a habit of mind and heart that enables the ordained person to 'delight in the law of the Lord' and 'on his law ... meditate day and night'(Ps 1...2); to 'pray always in the spirit' (Eph 6...18); to join himself and those in his pastoral care to Jesus Christ whose priestly work in heaven consists, according to the letter to the Hebrews, in always interceding for us (Heb 7:25); an interceding that is not a postscript to his priesthood, but rather its continual active presence before the Father, since Christ's priestly mediation and intercession are 'perpetual'(Heb 7:24). The man ordained in his name must develop a way of centering on that interceding that becomes the habit of mind and heart of the 'mystic'.

This habit of mind and heart regards what one is as more important than what one does; it allows the mustard seed to grow into all one's own being before it grows out to the world. The same habit of mind allows the eucharist, the mystery of faith, to be the summit and source of all preaching of the gospel (*PO* 15) and indeed of all pastoral action. Every moment of a eucharist well celebrated will resonate with people's lives in Church and world. The one presiding over it will be much more than one who recites sacramental words in a multiplicity of sacramental actions. Concern for the Word will be his full-time and all-absorbing existence; in the spirit of the prophet he will 'feed on' the word and be 'fed' by it (Ezek 3:1-3). He will be at all times ruminating, always pondering, always musing, always searching, always wondering how the Word can become flesh now. He will at all times try to live and act 'in the person of Christ,' with heart, lips and hands in Christ-filled harmony with every man and woman who is called to be Christ's face, Christ' presence, Christ's voice.

Notes

1   Cf K. Untener's article in *Worship*, January 1991.

2   Notably Bd. Marliangeas, *Clés pour une Théologie du Ministère*, Beauchesne, 1978.

3   Cf Sara Butler in *Worship*, May 1991.

4   e.g. in *LG* par 48.

5   Cf Charles R. Meyer in *Worship*, May 1991.

6   'Prosopology' deals with various aspects of the movements of the human face.

7   Cf C. Meyer.

8   John A.T. Robinson, *Honest to God*, 1963.

9   It is interesting that the word 'house,' *oikos*, is at the heart of five much used words: economy (of salvation), ecology, ecumenism, parochial, diocesan.

10   Shakespeare, Sonnet 97.

11   *Concilium*, 3, No 5.

12   Cf G. Tavard, *A Theology for Ministry*, Dominican Publications, 1983, p 149.

13   Pope John Paul II gives much attention to the topic of pastoral charity in *Pastores Dabo Vobis*, 1992.

14   An expression which gained much prominence in medieval Church writing, especially in Aquinas. Cf Marliangeas, pp 103-140.

15   M. Evans, 'In Persona Christi: The Key to Priestly Identity,' *Clergy Review*, April 1986, p 120.

16   Cf Sara Butler.

17   Cf H. Legrand, in *Worship*, November 1991.

18   Dryden, 'A Song for St Cecilia's Day'.

19   K. Rahner, *Theological Investigations*, VII, p 15.

What Difference
Does Priestly Ordination Make?

Brian M. Nolan

For over three centuries diocesan priesthood has conjured up the vision of a quite tightly organised group of ordained male celibates administering parishes at the behest of their bishops, who are subject to Rome. During the past thirty years or so, there has been a fresh appreciation of the Church as a mystery as well as an institution, of the local Church of the diocese and parish, of a wide variety of Church ministry, including that of the pope. The priesthood has sometimes been renamed the presbyterate, marking its character of community leadership; and the ordination rite was revised in 1968 to take account of this communitarian perspective. And of course there are voices in favour of women priests and married priests.

These eight areas of development will not all be treated below with equal attention. But since they interact, some attention will be given to each. The focus will be on the role of diocesan presbyters/ priests, and their collaboration with other baptised ministers. The main perspective will be the light shed by the new ordination rite to service of a local Church, which is marked by a network of local communities, and is in conscious communion with other local diocesan Churches. This exposition will include observations on Church ministry in general, and the Petrine and presbyteral ministries in particular. It will end with some reflections on possible consequences of the foregoing on the presbyteral ordination of women and married priests in a collegial Church of trinitarian communion.

1. The Church of God the Father, Son and Holy Spirit
Presbyterate/Priesthood is indubitably a service in and to the Church. Consequently, in order to determine the difference ordination makes, we must first clarify our notion of Church. During al-

most one thousand years the operative model for the Latin Church was that of an institutional pyramid with the Roman Pontiff at the apex, then, in descending order, the hierarchy, the priests, male religious, female religious, lay men, lay women, and finally children. Ordained ministry was deemed an empowerment, placing the recipients in a position of giving rather than receiving from or sharing with, the majority of the faithful. During this century the Roman Catholic Church was led to re-focus its self-image, mainly by various developments in western society. These changes included universal suffrage and education, democratisation replacing monarchical government, increasing appreciation of cultural diversity, the growing acceptance of human rights as well as duties, the entrance of women into professional and political life, the mobility and migration of peoples, the loosening of family discipline, and the transformation of rural and urban lifestyles.

Vatican II proposed an ecclesiology of the Church bodying forth the communion of our Triune God. The Church is the People of God (the Father) the Body of Christ (the Son), and the Temple of the Holy Spirit.[1] We began to notice the self-consciousness of the eastern Church, summed up by the living martyr from Romania, Dumitru Staniloaë: 'The church is the dialogue of God [the Father] with believers through Christ and in the Holy Spirit.'[2] Quite simply, *our Church enables us to live the life of our Triune God in our present situation.*

The equality of the three divine Persons founds the equality of believers by baptism into the people of God. Their personal identity as Father, Son and Holy Spirit, through their interrelationships, is mirrored in the individuating charisms for Church service granted to all members of the Body of Christ, and activated by confirmation. And the loving reciprocity that binds the Father, Son and Spirit into mutual life grounds the fellowship, the koinonia, of the eucharist. Every Christian is initiated by these three Church actions of baptism, confirmation, and eucharist and is thereby wholly equal, distinct, and mutual - like our Triune God. [3]

All are equal and in solidarity in the People of God the Father on the journey through time. All are different and complementary in the one charismatic Body of Christ. All are coaxed into sharing and serving by the empowering Spirit. The trinitarian fellowship of the Church means we are co-responsible and reciprocal. Diversity is enrichment, not a threat.[4] Selfless interaction is a divine necessity for us.[5]

2. *The Church as communion of communions: diocese and parish*

The local diocesan Church is not a part or a member of the Church universal. It is the manifestation in an area of the integral church of Christ, because it has everything it needs to celebrate the eucharistic paschal meal. The local Churches are like living cells, each containing the whole mystery of the one body of the Church. United with their pastors they are:

> in their own localities, the new people called by God, in the power of the Holy Spirit and as the result of full conviction (cf 1 Thess 1:5). In them the faithful are gathered together through the preaching of the Gospel of Christ, and the mystery of the Lord's Supper is celebrated 'so that, by means of the flesh and blood of the Lord the whole brotherhood of the Body may be welded together.'[6]

The whole Church of Christ is realised in the network of local Churches brought into being by the four factors mentioned above. The *Holy Spirit* of the risen Christ enlivens the evangelists preaching the *gospel*, which forms a fellowship of believers able to celebrate the *eucharist* of the kingdom in communion with their *pastor*, their bishop. The Spirit builds up each particular Church by bestowing charisms on each of the baptised-confirmed-eucharistised, and by inspiring them to mission and ministry. As the Spirit of diversity and yet of bonding in the Triune God, it both cherishes local traditions and individuality (see LG 13, 23 end; AG 4, 10, 15, 22), and develops collegiality by pastoral councils (CD 27), laity councils (Decree on the Apostolate of Lay People, AA 26), diocesan, provincial and national synods (CD 36), and the universal synod of bishops (CD 5). The gospel is a transforming message of judgment, reconciliation and joy, as well as a compelling image of Jesus Christ attracting to a new way of life. The bishop is not a delegate of the pope.[7] The 1983 Code of Canon Law does not view dioceses and parishes as administrative parts of a single world Church, but as independent subjects of Church life and law. The local Church is a complete, if interdependent, embodiment of the Church universal. Finally, epicletic Spirit, proclaimed gospel, and preaching pastor interact in eucharistic fellowship. 'The Church reveals herself most clearly when a full complement of God's holy people ... exercises a thorough and active participation at the very altar where the bishop presides in the company of his priests and other assistants.' (SC 41)

If the diocesan-local Church has been the subject of recent theological reflection,[8] the parish is the micro-Church most familiar to presbyters and people alike, and yet it has not received the attention it deserves.[9] Canon 515 provides a concise description: '§1 A parish is a certain community of Christ's faithful stably established within a particular Church, whose pastoral care, under the authority of the diocesan Bishop, is entrusted to a parish priest as its proper pastor.' A parish is a community before it is an area.[10] It is in its own way a communion of communions, if a pastoral team exercises co-responsibility, and works with, let us say, a financial and pastoral council and various committees, whose members ply various ministries. In some parts of the world the territorial boundaries of a parish are being crossed by movements such as the neo-catechumenate, lay institutes, religious orders, as well as by small Christian communities which are self-ministering, self-supporting, and self-propagating. Only by living as a cell of the local Church will the parish learn to interact with such movements and communities, whose very existence is welcomed by an ecclesiology of communion. Such a parish configuration may be represented as follows:[11]

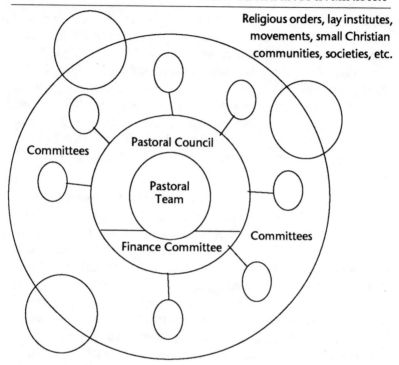

Religious orders, lay institutes, movements, small Christian communities, societies, etc.

Pastoral Council

Committees

Pastoral Team

Finance Committee

Committees

These seemingly anodyne descriptions of the local diocesan Churches and parish actually represent a paradigm shift in our understanding of the Catholic Church.[12] No longer is it viewed as a jurisdictional monolith under central control from Rome, or as a 'perfect society' independent of state, race, and culture. The universal Church exists only in local Churches, which are rooted in various situations and cultures, and live from interaction with them. Each local diocesan Church has a responsibility for the great Church, and for the unevangelised of the globe. It has its necessary contribution to make from its own vitality, which must be shared in ways still being developed – parochial, presbyteral and lay councils; pastoral consultations; diocesan synods and regional conferences of bishops; and universal synods.[13] 'This multiplicity of local Churches, unified in a common effort, shows all the more resplendently the catholicity of the undivided Church ... the whole Mystical Body ... is a corporate body of churches.' (LG 23; cf LG 13; AG 22)

3. Church Ministry

In the light of the foregoing considerations, it is hardly surprising that Pope John Paul II sketches an ecclesiology of the trinitarian communion of the local Churches, and even of the parish, before treating of the diverse charisms for service of the unordained, in *Christifideles Laici* (December 30, 1988), §§18-20 and 25-26. The following annotated description summarises Church ministry (as distinct from human or even Christian ministry). [14]

Church ministry is a believer's public activity,	An active, demanding work, not a godly disposition or passive state (like suffering), rendering the church visibly effective.
recognised in various ways by the (local) Church as Christlike and performed on her behalf,	Thus ecclesial (not sheerly personal) approval, installation, or ordination;[15] all ministry is rooted in Jesus Christ;[16] officially representative and supported.
directed to extend the kingdom of the Father and to upbuild the Christian community.	Church ministry 'names grace', cooperates with the Father shaping the world, and benefits the body of believers as well as others.
Such ministry is a gift, a charism from the Spirit of Jesus the Son, first proclaimed and celebrated by a believer in baptism-confirmation-eucharist (and by a few in ordination),	This ministry is grounded in Christian initiation and the universal prophetic, pastoral, and priestly roles bestowed by the risen Christ through his Spirit; all Christians are joyfully empowered to active witness as Church-persons[17] – there is no clerical monopoly.
having its own identity and indicated limits within a Church-communion, an interactive diversity of charisms of service.	The nature and number of ministries expand and contract over the centuries:[18] pluralism is normal; no one is omni-competent; all are interdependent.

4. The Petrine Ministry

The foregoing picture of a trinitarian communion of local diocesan and parochial Churches, and of a universal charismatic Church ministry, sheds light on the function of the pope. About one hundred and fifty years ago the Roman Pontiff began to exercise more explicit and detailed oversight of a rapidly expanding Roman Catholic Church. Previously, in a Eurocentric Church (outside the Papal States), bishops normally had been proposed locally by concordat with the civil power or by cathedral chapters, and they were nearly always approved by Rome.[19] This was not necessarily good for the local Church. Nor was it in accord with the earliest practice as instanced by the *Apostolic Tradition* of Hippolytus (about AD 230): 'Let him be ordained as bishop who has been chosen by all the people,' and by the pope who sent St Patrick to Ireland, St Celestine I (422-432), 'Let a bishop not be imposed upon the people whom they do not want.'[20] (And it was the same Celestine who, in his correspondence and through his legates at the Council of Ephesus, 'repeatedly asserted, with an unprecedented insistence, the pope's claim, as successor and living representative of St Peter, to paternal oversight of the entire Church, eastern no less than western.' [21]

The loss of the Papal States intensified a personal regard for the pope, whom Frederick William Faber had already declared to be, after Jesus and Mary, 'a third visible presence of Jesus amongst us … He is the visible shadow cast by the Invisible Head of the Church in the Blessed Sacrament.' Pius IX (1846-1878), a remarkable 'Vicar of Christ,'[22] was known by Monsignor George Talbot to labour long over his encyclicals and allocutions, 'and as the Pope is no great theologian himself, I feel convinced that when he writes them he is inspired by God.' [23]

Vatican II may have revised any notion of the Church as a papal monarchy, but it made little progress in organically relating the body of bishops with the pope, or showing how papal infallibility may not be divorced from the infallibility of the Church as a whole. Contemporary ecclesiologists generally work from the position of the Church being a communion of communions, a global network of interlocking local Churches served by the Petrine ministry. This ministry recognises true local Churches and their bishops; coordinates, encourages, and challenges them; and authenticates teaching and practice.[24] The present pope has said he insistently prays the Holy Spirit for enlightenment in the common eastern and western search for 'the forms in which this [Petrine] ministry may accomplish a service of love recognised by all concerned.'[25] Whatever exposition of the papal function may emerge, it may be legitimately portrayed as a most significant exercise of the ecclesial ministry described in the previous section.

5. The Presbyteral Ministry

The millennial image of the priest-sacrificer was exalted by the catechism for pastors commissioned by the Council of Trent, and produced in 1566, mainly by three Dominican theologians. Part II, Chapter VII, Question II, asserts that 'No dignity on earth excels the Order of the Priesthood' (not even the episcopate!):

> For as bishops and priests are as certain interpreters and heralds of God, who in his name teach men the divine law and the precepts of life, and are the representatives on earth of God himself, it is clear that their function is such, that none greater can be conceived; wherefore they are justly called not only 'angels' (Mal 2:7), but also 'gods' (Ps 81:6), holding as they do amongst us the power and authority of the immortal God ... [T]he priests of the new testament far exceed all others in honour; for the power of consecrating and offering the body and blood of our Lord, and of remitting sins, which had been conferred on them, transcends human reason and intelligence, still less can there be found on earth anything equal and like to it. [26]

This sense of the priest as set apart to offer Mass continued for some four hundred years:

> Vested in hallowed robes of rare tradition,
> I shall bow down before the Host of Praise,
> Speaking the Loveliest Thing in priestly mission,
> Doing the Loveliest Deed by one tense phrase. [27]

For some it must have been a surprise that the theological commission of Vatican II refused to accept the formulation that the priest's role is 'to join the spiritual sacrifice of men to the sacrifice of Christ in the eucharist,' on the grounds that the faithful do this for themselves![28]

The fresh perspective on the priesthood mainly derives from a retrieval of the praxis of the first Christian centuries. The focus has shifted from the crucified Jesus to the risen Christ. Christ is truly risen because he inaugurated the reign of his beloved Father through his ministry as prophet, king, and priest. Because the Head of the Church is ascended to the Father, he can send the Spirit of them both to constitute the community and movement he instituted. Christ now lives corporately in his Church. It is that ecclesial, Spirit-imparting Christ whom presbyters represent. Therefore, every presbyter is necessarily *from, in, and for a local Church*.[29]

The following description of a priest/presbyter attempts to express the christological, pneumatological, and ecclesiological dimensions, while following the pattern of the presbyter being (a) *from*, (b) *in*, and (c) *for a particular Church*.

(a) A presbyter is a member of a local Church who is discerned by an appropriate procedure to be particularly apt to represent Christ as Head of that Church, in communion with other recognised ministers, especially the bishop.

(b) This Church member is empowered to represent stably that Church to Christ, and Christ to that Church, by a charism of the Holy Spirit,[30] which is granted sacramentally through the ordered and ordering ministry of the assembled celebrating Church.[31]

(c) This charism enables the presbyter to minister to Christ in, with, and through that Church by evangelising the community as faithful prophet, by shepherding them as servant-king, and by celebrating with them as animating priest, delighting in the Father through the Spirit of his Son.[32]

6. The Rite of Presbyteral Ordination

The foregoing trinitarian communion ecclesiology of dioceses and parishes, the exposition of Church and Petrine ministry, and the description of a priest/presbyter as an official pastoral leader from, in, and for a local Church, may now be tested against a prime theological statements of the difference ordination makes – the rite of ordination to the presbyterate.

Ordination (whether episcopal, presbyteral or diaconal) is a worship action of a local Church to realise its potential to body forth Christ, by designating and presenting to the Spirit of Christ persons considered apt to focus, symbolise, and activate the baptismal priesthood of the community by stimulating and coordinating its charisms.[33] The Christ who is active in the ordination, and whom, as Head, the presbyter specifically represents, is the Christ embodied in that praying local Church.[34] Thus ordination associates the presbyter intimately with the assembly.

Firstly, presbyteral ordination is a process initiated by the local Church, coming *from the local Church*. There is the community's discernment both of the need for a pastoral minister, and of the aptitude for it of a particular candidate. The local Church calls and presents the candidates: 'Those to be ordained priests please come forward'; 'Most Reverend Father, holy mother [local?] Church asks you to ordain these men, *our brothers*, for service as priests.' The ordaining bishop inquires about those to be admitted to the presbyteral college: 'Do *you* judge them to be worthy?' There is afterwards his scrutiny: 'Are you resolved, with the help of the Holy Spirit, ... to be fellow workers with the bishops in caring for the Lord's flock ... to celebrate the mysteries of Christ ... to consecrate your life to God for the salvation of his people?' The discernment, call and scrutiny of the candidates are crowned by the consent of the worshipping assembly: 'Thanks be to God!' The form of that assent suggests that this is no modern democratic election of ministers, but the gracious symbiosis of the discernment from below of the divine choice of the candidates from above. [35]

The ordination is equally a rite unfolding *in the local Church*. The presbyteral order is mentioned five times, driving home that the newly ordained is a member of an ecclesial group, the diocesan presbyterium. The vertical dimension of the presbyterate (and *a for-*

tiori of the episcopate) is its apostolicity, its stretching back in time
to the very mission and ministry of Jesus and his first followers.
The homily brings this out: 'Our High Priest, Jesus Christ, … was
sent by the Father, and he in turn sent the apostles into the world;
through them and their successors, the bishops, he continues his
work as Teacher, Priest and Shepherd. Priests are co-workers of the
order of bishops.' The horizontal, world-embracing dimension of
the presbyterate is conveyed by its catholicity proclaimed in the final words of the Prayer of Consecration: 'May they be faithful in
working with the order of bishops, so that the words of the gospel
may reach the ends of the earth, and the family of nations, made
one in Christ, may become God's one, holy people.' Ecclesial collegiality, apostolicity and catholicity are focused in the bishop and
presbyters. They symbolise in different degrees ordered colleges
existing at the intersection of apostolicity conquering time and of
catholicity overcoming the dispersion of space. That makes them
different from the faithful practising the priesthood of baptism,
who do not strongly symbolise the 'cross' formed by vertical apostolicity and horizontal catholicity. The ordained are, therefore, a
special 'cross people' inserting the local Church into the universal
Church founded on the apostles. But the assembly has its necessary
voice in the conferral of this creative symbolism on official Church
persons, the ordained leaders. The worshipping local Church
prays, 'The Lord be with you,' and responds, especially in the Litany
of the Saints, to the presider's 'Let us pray.' The central episcopal
Prayer of Consecration receives a resounding 'Amen!' There is a
note of congregational thanksgiving for the pneumatic gifts of ordained ministries, and of intercession for those being ordained.[36]
The Litany concludes with, 'Hear us, Lord our God, and pour out
upon these servants of yours the blessing of the Holy Spirit, and the
grace and power of the priesthood. In your sight we offer these
men for ordination: support them with your unfailing love.' Neither the assembly nor the bishop confer the Holy Spirit. They ask
for the bestowal of the Holy Spirit, and they ask in the Spirit. [37]

Thirdly, the presbyteral ordination is celebrated *for the local Church*,
since it has a claim to the ministry of the ordained. Up to this day in

the east, and until about the twelfth century in the Latin west, the candidates for presbyterate had to be assigned to a specific Church (i.e., parish), shrine, monastery, or other definite pastoral function. Ordination was also normally first installation.[38] The rite repeatedly mentions the threefold pastoral ministry of the presbyter. The Homily says, 'He is to serve Christ the Teacher, Priest, and Shepherd in his ministry which is to make his own body, the Church, grow into the people of God ... to lead them effectively, through Christ and in the Holy Spirit, to God the Father.' Finally, it is for the sake of the Church, local and universal (*Pastores Dabo Vobis*, §§31-32), that the presbyter is sealed by the Spirit, the character of Order, and required 'to consecrate your life to God for the salvation of his people, and to unite yourself more closely every day to Christ the High Priest'; and 'Imitate the mystery you celebrate: model your life on the mystery of the Lord's cross.' [39]

The setting of the ordination rite is richly symbolic of its meaning. It is part of a local Church eucharist (and originally the Sunday eucharist) where the whole 'assembly itself is the primary and most fundamental celebrant of liturgy ... When it is duly constituted, the assembly is the outstanding sign of the presence of Christ to his Church.'[40] The eucharist provides the necessary context of a local Church ministering to itself in its proper order, namely, those ordained by baptism-confirmation exercising their appropriate 138roles, interacting with the presider in the episcopal or presbyteral order.[41] The assembly actively remembers,through the Holy Spirit and with the risen Christ, Jesus' table fellowship and sharing of life even unto death. Since the eucharist is the action of the whole community, presbyteral ordination is seen as insertion into the life of the Body of Christ, rather than as giving the presbyter unique and individual power to consecrate the bread and   wine.[42]

The ordination takes place after the proclamation of the Scriptural word, indicating that the assembly – including the ordained – are the servants, not the masters, of this word. Since lay readers and lay preaching are reviving in the Catholic Church, presbyters will in time be understood as sharing in, if directing, the ministry of the word.

The 1968 revision of the ordination rite heightens the traditional emphasis on the essential invocation of the Holy Spirit on the candidates among and by the assembled, ordered local Church. But it retains sacerdotalist imagery in the references to the levitical priesthood during the prayer of consecration, despite the return to the original secular title of service to and oversight of the community, 'presbyter.' The retention, but downgrading, of the anointing of the hands, the vesting, and the bestowal of the symbols of office (though the bread and cup are to be accepted 'from the holy people of God'), preserves a doubtful sense of hierarchy. This sacerdotalism and hierarchicalism could in future be balanced, indeed replaced, by actions symbolising the solidarity of the presbyter with the assembly. For instance, procedures could be evolved for organising a broadly based, informed and serious assent of the local Church to the ordination. The promise of obedience to the bishop could be paralleled by a public commitment to consult and collaborate with the presbyterium and the faithful. If the powerful ones in the early Church were the martyrs, the publicly and decisively marginalised, then the faith-filled weak of this world and its outsiders should have their power before God symbolised in the rite. Believers who may have been neglected include women, the poor, the young, the sick, the handicapped the uneducated, the unemployed, immigrants, prisoners, and minorities. Their authority should be acknowledged as contributing to the ordering of the Church. The beatitudes of Jesus, Paul at Corinth (1 Cor 1:22-31), and the very sign of the cross, warn us that the ordering of the Church is normally counter-cultural. [43]

7. Implications for the Presbyteral Ordination of Women

The title of this essay, 'What difference does priestly ordination make?' may now be altered to 'What difference could priestly ordination make?' This suggests that a renewed pneumatological and ecclesiological understanding of Church ministry and ordination may speak to current questions such as the ordination of women and presbyteral celibacy. But these concluding two sections are in the nature of appendices. The treatment will be appropriately tentative.

At the outset a distinction must be made. Are we to consider the presbyterate a profession or a vocation? If it is just a worthy profession of community service, then there can hardly be any objection to the admission of women to the presbyterium or the episcopacy. But if the presbyterate is viewed as a vocation, a spiritual charism, then we cannot automatically say the Spirit graces both women and men. We must look to the christological dimension, and examine if the maleness of Jesus Christ is theologically normative for entry to the presbyterate. There were cultural reasons for the failure to address this problem. Beginning in the second half of the first century, the presbyterate became sociologically domesticated as first a neo-levitical, and then an imperial, public function and social rank. The priestly and hierarchical categories did not allow the possibility of women presbyters to arise. Until the second half of this century (with apparently the minor exception of Southern Italy and Sicily in the time of Gelasius I, 494), no significant attention was given to the matter. To compress a vast amount of scholarly research and publication, this writer is of the view that there is nothing in Scripture, or Church tradition and practice, or the magisterium, definitively excluding women from the presbyterate or episcopate.

The single theological difficulty[44] persisting, in the view of this writer, is the elucidation of what it means to be a woman or a man in Christ. It is possible that the – largely unexamined – practice of the Church of both east and west of admitting only men to the presbyterate may intuitively capture a deep insight into Christian anthropology, which might preclude the ordination of women.[45] However, the presbyter is a representative, not a representation, of Christ.[46] This weakens arguments in favour of gender limitation of ordained ministry. Another factor in any possible change of discipline is the realisation percolating through the body of believers that the ordained act in the person of Christ the Head, but as ecclesially discerned members of the local Church, which embodies that Christ in the Holy Spirit. Therefore, to act in the person of Christ is equally to act in the name of the Church, which is Christ in his current existence, rather than to act in the name of the Jesus of Palestine, or of the Sermon on the Mount, or of the cross, or even of the Easter Christ before Pentecost.[47] Since women can represent 'holy mother Church', they should be able to represent the ecclesial Christ in the order of presbyterate or episcopacy.

The foregoing expresses points and pointers. There is much opening of the heart and eyes needed. At least three fields of vital experience must be integrated: that of women worldwide, that of other Churches (including the Orthodox Churches, so staunchly defensive of a male presbyterate), and that of other cultures where the Church is rooted. In addition to this programme, the actual practice of order, as pastoral ministry in the name and person of the ecclesial Christ, must be allowed flourish in a Spirit-fired trinitarian communion Church. Symbols are necessarily polyvalent and operative at the intuitive and affective levels, as well as the more logical. The symbolism of women presbyters may be more effective in the twenty-first century than it would have been in the first (or the twentieth).

8. Implications for presbyteral celibacy

Probably even from the earliest decades after Pentecost, some apostles practised abstinence from marital relations while on mission; note 1 Cor 7:8, 32 35, but also 9:5. Church legislation mandating total abstinence from sexual intercourse for married bishops and priests, or perpetual celibacy for the unmarried, is early in the western Church.[48] The Council of Carthage in 390 proposes priestly celibacy as intensifying intercession. Availability for ministry as a motive is very rarely used in early Church documents.[49] Occasionally, even in the early Church, celibacy was portrayed as marriage to the Church and spiritual fatherhood (e.g. Origen and Gregory the Great). There is no gainsaying that celibacy was a striking way for presbyters and bishops to incarnate Jesus, the independent prophet and self-sacrificing shepherd. The reasons given for celibacy may not always have been nobly cogent, but it is clearly a special kind of ministerial loving, whereby the family-less one calls the faithful into their future absorption into the kingdom of God.[50] There are testimonies to celibacy 'happening' to ordained ministers and candidates, just as any person falls in love. There is more than the rational and calculating. Here is a pulse of real being.

The sacerdotalist image of 'priesthood' emphasised the separation of the presbyter from the believing community. Celibacy is especially fitting to express that apartness, and dedication to the Church. It will always be so. But in recent decades presbyters are increasingly being understood as inserted into the local Church, in whose name they act. Secondly, the theology of sexuality and marriage is more optimistic and holistic then ever before. How strange it is that the sacrament of the pneumatisation of interpersonal relations, and a source of fruitfulness of the Church, has no reference to the Triune God in its ritual (apart from the sign of the cross at the exchange of rings). This is very different from the eastern Church, where the trinitarian presbyteral blessing and witness, not the consent of the partners, makes the marriage. The perichoresis of marriage is gradually being experienced as a way of being a micro-Church, a trinitarian communion.

The same communion of communions ecclesiology is beginning to root ordained ministry in the panoply of interacting and complementary charisms that bring the local Church into being. 'The Church is primarily *communion*, i.e. a set of relationships making up a mode of being, exactly as is the case in the Trinitarian God.'[51] The charism of celibacy has served well the image of the Church as a universal institution growing towards the eschaton, when there will be neither marrying nor giving in marriage. The charism of marriage could provide a different, yet appropriate, witness for a presbyter serving a Church of trinitarian perichoresis, in which the eschatological Spirit is already powerfully at work healing and drawing together.

Conclusion
The road we travelled may have seemed tortuous, but many places had to be visited in order to establish a satisfactory itinerary. The Church was viewed as an organism, a trinitarian communion of interacting particular Churches. The diocese is a self-sufficient, if interdependent, local Church in communion with all others throughout the globe. The parish is a miniature Church. It too is a

communion of communions, with its parish council and committees, its constellation of recognised ministers, and perhaps small
Christian communities of various kinds crossing the parish boundaries. Church ministry belongs to all Christians, and is often spok-
en alongside of, and even including, the ordained ministry. Indeed,
it may possibly embrace the Petrine coordinating and approving
ministry. Priesthood is renamed the collegiate presbyterate, imply-
ing the commissioning by an ordered and ordering liturgical assembly to collaborative leadership of word, pastoral charity and
celebration. Presbyteral ordination projects the image of an epicletic, sacramental authorisation by, in and for a local Church, to evan-
gelise, form and animate a Christian community. Service of the ecclesial Christ through his Spirit is the keynote, and not a
communication of power. The first world is under steady cultural
pressure to re-examine its tradition (or custom?) of admitting only
males to the presbyterate. There is need of much study and observation here. In its hunger for the eucharist, the third world sometimes requests the ordination of some worthy local Catholic leaders
who happen to be married. Here, and elsewhere in our Church of
trinitarian communion, new vistas are opening up. Fresh possibilities invite us into a future which may have many of the Church
characteristics of the first three centuries of our era.

Notes:

1.   See Vatican II Dogmatic Constitution on the Church, LG 17;
     and Decrees on the Church's Missionary Activity, AG 7, and on
     the Ministry and Life of Priests, PO 1. LG opens by describing
     the roles in the church of the Father (§2), the Son (§3), and the
     Holy Spirit (§4), and concludes with a phrase of St Cyprian of
     Carthage (d. 258), 'Hence the universal church is seen to be 'a
     people brought into unity from the unity of the Father, the Son
     and the Holy Spirit" (§4; and cf. §§17, 26). Note the trinitarian
     character of the Church's ecumenical appeal in UR 2, 15; of its
     missionary outreach in in AG 2-4; of its local realisation in the

Decree on the Pastoral Office of Bishops in the Church (CD 11); and of its continuing vitality in PO 1 and the Pastoral Constitution on the Church in the Modern World, GS 24 and 40.

2. D Staniloaë, *Le génie de l'Orthodoxie: Introduction* (Collection 'Théophanie'; Paris, Desclée de Brouwer, 1985, p 78. On trinitarian ecclesiology see Robert Kress, *The Church: Communion, Sacrament, Communication*, New York, Paulist Press, 1985, pp 30-160, esp pp 30-36 and 65-72; Edward J Kilmartin SJ, *Christian Liturgy: Theology and Practice. I. Systematic Theology of Liturgy*, Kansas City, Sheed & Ward, 1988, pp 222-228; Colin E Gunton, *The Promise of Trinitarian Theology*, Edinburgh, T & T Clark, 1991, chap 4, 'The Community: The Trinity and the Being of the Church,' pp 55-85; Catherine Mowry LaCugna, *God For Us: The Trinity and Christian Life*, San Francisco, Harper, 1991, pp 401-403.

3. The First Statement of the Joint Commission for Theological Dialogue Between the Roman Catholic Church and the Orthodox Church deals with the *Church, Eucharist, Trinity: The Mystery of the Church and of the Eucharist in the Light of the Holy Trinity*, issued in 1982, London, CTS, 1984, pp 16. Before speaking of the ministry of the bishop, the Commission states on p 10:

This mystery of the unity in love of many persons constitutes the real newness of the Trinitarian koinonia [fellowship] communicated to men in the Church through the eucharist. Such is the purpose of Christ's saving work, which is spread abroad in the last times after Pentecost.

This is why the Church finds its model, its origin and its purpose in the mystery of God, one in three persons ... The institutional elements should be nothing but a visible reflection of the reality of the mystery.

4. 'The non-violent style of the trinity and its life of unity respectful of differences gives directional clues to the church for its style of ministry for justice,' John A Coleman SJ, 'The Mission of the Church and Action on Behalf of Justice,' *The Jurist* 39 (1979), 119-151, at p 132.

Many reflect on practical conclusions from a trinitarian ecclesiology, e.g., Leonardo Boff (*Trinity and Society*, Tunbridge
Wells, Burns & Oates, 1988, pp 22-23:

[A] church, inspired by the communion of the Trinity, would
be characterised by a more equitable sharing of sacred power,
by dialogue, by openness to all the charisms granted to the
members of the community, by the disappearance of all types
of discrimination, especially those originating in patriarchal-
ism and *machismo*, by its permanent search for a consensus to
be built up through the organised participation of all its
members.

Similarly C M LaCugna (*God For Us*, 402-403).

5.   The intercommunion essential to the unity of the three divine
     Persons allows them to draw life from each other. Perichoresis
     is the term given since the eighth century to this affirming
     interaction. It has often been compared to a similar sounding
     word meaning an interweaving dance, in this case performed
     by the three divine Persons utterly responsive to each other.
     See further in C M LaCugna, *God For Us*, 270-278; L. Boff, *Trinity
     and Society*, 134-148 (theology) and 148-154 (implications for
     human societies).

6.   LG 26; cf Avery Dulles SJ, *The Catholicity of the Church*, Oxford,
     Clarendon, 1985, pp 133-134, 136-138; Patrick Granfield, 'The
     Church Local and Universal: Realisation of Communion,' *The
     Jurist* 49 (1989), 449-471, esp pp 454-457.

7.   See *LG* 27 and J M R Tillard OP, *The Bishop of Rome*, London,
     SPCK, 1983, pp 150-157. Trent saw only a greater jurisdiction
     distinguishing a bishop from a priest. Vatican II provided the
     first formal clarification that episcopacy is a sacramental order;
     cf Susan Wood SCL, 'The Sacramentality of Episcopal Con-
     secration,' *Theological Studies* 51 (1990), 479-496. The very close
     association of episcopacy with jurisdiction, and the consequent
     control of benefices and revenues, helps to explain why during
     the century and a half before the Reformation only one of the
     'bishops' of Strasbourg went so far as to be ordained even a

priest (but not a bishop), according to Louis Bouyer in Peter Moore, ed, *Bishops But What Kind? Reflections on Episcopacy*, London, SPCK, 1982, p 31.

8.   For example, Herve Legrand, 'L'Eglise se réalise en un lieu,' in Bernard Lauret and François Refoulé, eds, *Initiation à la pratique de la théologie, Tome III: Dogmatique 2*, Paris, Le Cerf, 1983, pp 145-180; John D Zizioulas, *Being as Communion: Studies in Personhood and the Church*, London, DLT, 1985, chap 7, 'The Local Church in a Perspective of Communion,' pp 247-260; P. Granfield, 'The Church Local and Universal.'

9.   See the Constitution on the Sacred Liturgy, *SC* 42; H. Legrand, 'L'Eglise,' 174-176; Gerald A Arbuckle SM, *Earthing the Gospel: An inculturation handbook for pastoral workers*, London, Chapman, 1990, pp 79-95; William J Rademacher, *Lay Ministry: A Theological, Spiritual, and Pastoral Handbook*, Slough, St Paul Publications, 1991, pp 117-124 (giving ten 'main ecclesial elements' on p 1213. The topic is treated by Joseph F. McCann, C.M., *Church and Organization*, Scranton, University of Scranton Press, forthcoming.

10.   Note *Christifideles Laici* §26. Indeed, the diocese may be a cultural entity rather than a territorial one according to Allen Brent, *Cultural Episcopacy and Ecumenism: Representative Ministry in Church History from the Age of Ignatius of Antioch to the Reformation, With Special Reference to Contemporary Ecumenism*, Studies in Christian Mission 6, Leiden, E J Brill, 1992, esp pp 1-28 and 185-208. Canons 372 and 518 make it clear that neither the local diocesan nor the local parochial Church need be territorially defined. Distinctiveness of rite or language or nationality may call for a person-based local Church. This principle is capable of considerable development. The special needs of, for example, the armed forces and Opus Dei are already catered for by non-territorial bishops. Perhaps in time to come such categories as the unemployed, the addicted, the travelling people, and the physically challenged, may experience a new way of being the local Church gathered around their own bishop.

11. This diagram has been developed from one given by Jean Rigal, *Préparer l'avenir de l'Eglise*, Collection 'Théologies', Paris, Le Cerf, 1990, p 180.

12. Vatican II avoided 'Roman Catholic' and 'Roman Church', partly because this refers to the church in Rome; cf Avery Dulles, *The Catholicity of the Church*, 132-133. Paul VI signed the Vatican II decrees with 'Bishop of the Catholic Church', meaning the church at Rome (not of Rome), according to H Legrand, 'L'Eglise,' 317, n 224.

13. The Latin Church has a long way to go to deploy its local Church riches. Joseph A Komonchak concludes, 'On the level of theory, then, I am inclined to think that the question of the applicability of subsidiarity is not yet ripe for solution. Too many prior ecclesiological and sociophilosophical questions need to be identified and addressed first.' 'Subsidiarity in the Church: The State of the Question,' *The Jurist* 48, 1988, 298-349, at p 342.

14. The activities of the ordained and the unordained may be termed ministry: 'In the Church there is diversity of ministry but unity of mission ... [T]he laity are made to share in the priestly, prophetical and kingly office of Christ; they have therefore, in the Church and in the world, their own assignment in the mission of the whole People of God,' AA 2; cf AG 23; Elissa Rinere CP, 'Conciliar and Canonical Applications of "Ministry" to the Laity,' *The Jurist* 47, 1987, 204-227.

    The bibliography on Church ministry is enormous and flourishing. The following proved useful: Thomas Franklin O'Meara OP, *Theology of Ministry*, New York, Paulist Press, 1983, pp 136-161, esp pp 136 and 142; Joseph M Powers SJ, 'Ministry' in Peter E Fink SJ, ed, *The New Dictionary of Sacramental Worship*, Dublin, Gill and Macmillan, 1990, pp 828-837; and 'Ministry, Lay,' (Virginia S. Finn), pp 842-844; 'Ministry, Team,' (Dody H. Donnelly), pp 844-848; 'Ministry, Women in,' (Miriam D Ukeritis CSJ), pp 848-852; Michael G Lawler, *A Theology of Ministry*, Kansas City, Sheed & Ward, 1990, esp pp 20-35; W J Rademacher, *Lay Ministry*, esp pp 89-97.

15. The terminology for ecclesial recognition of ministries is still
     fluid. 'Approval' here means formal Church acknowledgment
     (which may or may not involve a commissioning ceremony or
     contract) of such leadership activities as pastoral assistant,
     chaplain to a hospital, school or prison, catechist, head of music,
     liturgist, youth leader, ecumenist, parish secretary, family or
     bereavement counsellor, faith friends, coordinators of groups
     for prayer, scripture study, or poor relief, hospitality giver,
     healer. 'Installation' requires a liturgical rite, and is currently
     limited to lector and acolyte (reader and eucharistic minister
     with a definitive commitment). 'Ordination' demands a sacra-
     mental rite for bishops, presbyters and deacons. Approval
     meets the changing demands of current mission. Installation
     denotes a significant institution associated with the community
     eucharistic assembly. Ordination is part of the sacramental
     structure of the Church guaranteeing catholicity and apostol-
     icity. See more below under 'The Presbyteral Ministry.'

16. The recovery by the western Church during recent decades of
     the ecclesiological context and pneumatological dynamism of
     all ministry should not downplay the scriptural and customary
     portrayal of ministers as 'other Christs,' despite the improper
     restriction of that title to priests for much of the last millenium
     in the West - a restriction avoided by the Decree on the Minis-
     try and Life of Priests §12, which terminates a quotation of Pius
     XI just before that phrase occurs for priests. See the helpful
     treatment by Kenan B Osborne OFM, *Priesthood: A History of the
     Ordained Ministry in the Roman Catholic Church*, New York,
     Paulist Press, 1988, esp pp 3-29, 317-318; and the more wide-
     ranging John F O'Grady, *Disciples and Leaders: The Origins of
     Christian Ministry in the New Testament*, New York, Paulist
     Press, 1991, pp 36-66, 85, 108-113; also in this work, Thomas
     Lane, 'Person, Presence, Face, Voice: A Context for Christian
     Ministry.'

17. See K B Osborne, *Priesthood*, 318-324, 338-340; and n 14 above.

18. Since this ministry is an official service of the Church to the
     kingdom of God, its variety and detailed structure will depend

on actual current needs and understanding of ecclesiology.
Theologians are uncertain if the threefold order of bishop, presbyter and deacon is strictly essential to the Church. It is significant that Vatican II would not declare the differentiation of the
single apostolic ministry into the three grades to be of divine
origin. This ministry was 'exercised in different degrees by
those who *even from ancient times* have been called bishops,
priests and deacons' (LG 28, stress added). Before Vatican II
(LG §§26 and 29) it was permissible to hold that the episcopate
and diaconate were not separate sacramental orders.

19. Cf J Derek Holmes, *The Triumph of the Holy See: A Short History
     of the Papacy in the Nineteenth Century*, London, Burns & Oates,
     1978, p 136. The Orthodox czars appointed the Latin bishops in
     their empire, according to Hervé-Marie Legrand, 'Theology
     and the Election of Bishops in the Early Church,' *Concilium* Vol
     7, No 8 (September 1972), 31-42, at p 32, n 3. Today a right of
     consultation about the candidates for sees is acknowledged for
     the governments of Austria, France, Germany, Poland, Port-
     ugal, Argentina, Colombia, Ecuador, and Venezuela, as noted
     by Thomas P Rausch SJ, *Authority and leadership in the Church:
     Past Directions and Future Possibilities*, Wilmington, Glazier,
     1989, p 146. The 1983 Code declares that the pope 'freely
     appoints Bishops or confirms those lawfully elected' (377 §1).
     The last phrase preserves some of the older arrangement.

20. Add St Leo the Great (440-461), who dubbed himself 'the prim-
     ate of all the bishops' since he was the successor of St Peter: 'He
     who has to preside over all must be elected by all.' These and
     other references are found in H-M Legrand, 'Theology and the
     Election of Bishops,' 33-34. However, it should be recalled that
     bishops in the early christian centuries, apart from the great
     urban sees, often resembled pastors of large parishes today.
     They might be expected to be known by many of the local faith-
     ful. Later, when dealing with presbyteral ordination, it will be
     indicated that episcopal elections were not a primitive democ-
     racy, but a discernment of charism, God's choice of this person
     for leadership.

21. J N D Kelly, *The Oxford Dictionary of Popes* (Oxford, OUP, 1986, p 42.

22. The title 'Vicar of Christ' (rather than 'Vicar of Peter') was seemingly first applied to Pope St Gelasius I in 495; see J N D Kelly, *The Oxford Dictionary of the Popes*, 48. It was later shared with bishops and priests until it was taken over by Innocent III (1198-1216); see Kelly, p 186. It is employed three times by Vatican II (LG §§18, 22; OT §9), which nowhere gives the pope a title inserting him into the local Church, whether regional (eg, 'the Patriarch of the West'), or diocesan ('the Bishop of Rome'); cf H Legrand, 'L'Eglise,' 316-317.

23. Both quotations are found in J Derek Holmes, *More Roman then Rome: English Catholicism in the Nineteenth Century*, London, Burns & Oates, 1978, pp 118 and 130 respectively.

24. See further in J Michael Miller CSB, *What Are They Saying About Papal Primacy?*, New York, Paulist Press, 1983; H Legrand, 'L'Eglise,' 275-329; J M R Tillard, *The Bishop of Rome*; A Dulles, *The Catholicity of the Church*, 134-146; Peter Drilling, *Trinity and Ministry*, Minneapolis, Augsburg Fortress, 1991, pp 132-141.

There is no real incompatibility between the following statements: 'The episcopality of the Roman primacy makes it - or rather should make it - symbolic of what all ministers must be in their service to the People of God' (George H Tavard, *A Theology for Ministry*, Theology and Life Series 6, Dublin, Dominican Publications, 1983, p 153); and, 'The Catholic Church sees ... in the primacy of the successors of Peter something positively intended by God and deriving from the will and institution of Jesus Christ' (Congregation for the Doctrine of the Faith and the Pontifical Council for the Promotion of Christian Unity, 'Response to ARCIC I Final Report,' *Origins* Vol 21, No 28, December 19, 1991, pp 441, 443-447, at p 445).

25. *L'Osservatore Romano* (English language edition), December 21-28, 1987, p 8 (as cited by P Drilling, *Trinity and Ministry*, 139 n 38).

26. J Donovan, translator, *The Catechism of the Council of Trent,* Dublin, James Duffy, no date [1829], p 275.

27. Benen, 'To-morrow (A young priest's First Mass),' in *The High Adventure. Poems Reprinted from 'The Far East'*, Chinese Mission Series, Galway, Dalgan Park, The Maynooth Mission to China, 1924, p 103.

28. Cf *Presbyterorum Ordinis 2, Expansio modorum,* pp 22-23: cited by Hervé-Marie Legrand OP, 'The Presidency of the Eucharist According to the Ancient Tradition,' *Worship* 53 (1979), 413-438, at p 434 n 65. Clarity is not yet attained. 'Roman documents subsequent to the reform of 1970 ... continue to be ambiguous as to the specific manner in which priest/presbyter, priest/concelebrant, and other members of the assembly participate in the local Church's eucharist,' Mary Alice Piil CSJ, 'The Local Church as the Subject of the Action of the Eucharist,' in Peter C Finn and James L Schellman, eds, *Shaping English Liturgy: Studies in Honor of Archbishop Denis Hurley,* Washington, The Pastoral Press, 1990, pp 173-196, at p 195.

29. Priests receive their mission and threefold ministry from Christ himself, through his Spirit, at their insertion into the presbyterium by ordination. Theologically speaking, it is not correct to call priests ministers of the Church. 'Rather, they act in the name of the Church, but they are really ministers of Christ himself' (K B Osborne, *Priesthood,* 331).

30. The medieval and later notions of the indelible character of Order imparting unique powers to absolve and consecrate the bread and wine tended to give priests the aura of superiority to the laity, prompting Luther to exclaim that the character was the ruin of Christian fraternity. It seems also to have contributed to a down-playing of evangelisation, preaching, and service of the poor (see n 38). A more rounded description of the character of Order is to identify it as the seal of the Spirit authenticating the ordained person's consecration to the Church and to Christ her Head, and simultanesously guaranteeing the acceptance and support of the local Church, and the authorisation to minister to her in the episcopal or presbyteral order.

Recent theology views the character of Order as covenantal, deepening the participation in the life of the Triune God and of the Church; cf Nathan Mitchell OSB, *Mission and Ministry: History and Theology in the Sacrament of Order*, Message of the Sacraments 6, Wilmington, Glazier, 1982, pp 306-308; J D Zizioulas, *Being as Communion*, 225-236; M G Lawler, *A Theology of Ministry*, 93-94; P Drilling, *Trinity and Ministry*, 73-82; John Paul II, *Pastores Dabo Vobis*, Post-Synodal Apostolic Exhortation on the Formation of Priests in the Circumstances of the Present Day (English text released April 7, 1992), in *Origins* Vol 21, No 45 (April 16, 1992), 717, 719-759, at §512 and 16 (pp 724, 725-726).

31. 'Priesthood of the faithful is as *member* of the Church; priesthood of the ordained as *sacrament* of the Church.' This formula is from Peter E Fink SJ, 'The Sacrament of Orders: Some Liturgical Reflections,' *Worship* 56 (1982), 482-502, at p 492. The ordained embody a community- structuring ministry with a wholetime dedication ratified by the local Church. This makes them symbols of that servanthood to which all the baptised aspire. The ordained summon the Church to be Church. They activate the universal priesthood of the baptised, and work together with them. See further Robert M Schwartz, *Servant Leaders of the People of God: An Ecclesial Spirituality for American Priests*, New York, Paulist Press, 1989, pp 125-132; Donald L Gelpi SJ, 'Priesthood,' *The New Dictionary of Sacramental Worship*, 1013-1018, at p 1018; John Thornhill SM, 'The Role of the Ordained Minister Within the Christian Community,' *The Australasian Catholic Record* lxvii (1990), 187-206; *Pastores Dabo Vobis*, §16 (p 725). As Michael G Lawler puts it, 'Ordained persons are called to everything to which ecclesial priests [the baptised] are called; they are called also to more, namely, to leadership in the name of the Church and, therefore, also in the name of Christ ... But only ordained priests are called and appointed to pastoral and liturgical leadership' (*A Theology of Ministry*, 64).

32. Archbishop Daniel Pilarczyk of Cincinnati offered a brief and clear definition of a priest in *Origins* Vol 20, No 19 (October 18,

1990), 'Defining the Priesthood,' pp 297, 299-300, at p 299 (in italics):

The priest is a member of the Christian faithful who has been permanently configured by Christ through holy orders to serve the Church, in collaboration with the local bishop, as representative and agent of Christ, the head of the Church, and therefore as representative and agent of the Church community before God and the world.

The description given by the present writer is less tied to received terminology ('permanently configured'), is more trinitarian and pneumatological, and is more explicitly rooted in the ministering local church. It is also closer to the ecumenical Lima declaration *Baptism, Eucharist and Ministry*, Faith and Order Paper no 111, Geneva, World Council of Churches, 1982, 'Ministry II, §§7-15,' on pp 21-22. Moreover, it echoes some elements of *Pastores Dabo Vobis* §§12, 16, 31.

Ministry is treated in a trinitarian perspective by G Greshake, *The Meaning of Christian Priesthood* (see n 47), 85-98; Mary M Schaefer and J Frank Henderson, *The Catholic Priesthood: A Liturgically Based Theology of the Presbyteral Office*, Canadian Studies in Liturgy No 4, Ottawa, CCCB Publications Service, 1990, pp 23-31; P Drilling, *Trinity and Ministry*, 33-42.

33.   Cf P E Fink, 'Ordination,' *A New Dictionary of Christian Theology*, eds. A Richardson and J Bowden, London, SCM, 1983, 418-420, at pp 418/1 and 420/1.

34.   P E Fink, 'The Sacrament of Orders,' 485-486.

35.   See G Greshake, *The Meaning of Christian Priesthood* (n 47), 94-97; Paul F Bradshaw, *Ordination Rites of the Ancient Churches of East and West*, New York, Pueblo Publishing Company, 1990, p 22.

36.   'The thanksgiving rejoices in the power of symbolic leadership, in the authority of one who can greet us in the Lord's name; the beseeching criticises that same leadership, pointing to the ordained as one in need of the community's prayers and

community's blessing,' Gordon W Lathrop, 'Christian Leadership and Liturgical Community,' *Worship* 66 (1992), 98-125, at p 118.

37. Francis A Sullivan SJ, (*The Church We Believe In: One, Holy, Catholic and Apostolic*, Dublin, Gill and Macmillan, 1988, p 180) writes, 'The ordaining bishop did not confer the Spirit; he had to pray that it be given, but with confidence that God had chosen the man who had been proposed and found acceptable by all.' '[T]he ordained in their ministry are placed at the disposal of God's Spirit. It is not the other way around.' (P E Fink, 'The Sacrament of Orders,' 490). The Spirit is bestowed not only on the ordinand: 'At the same time the Spirit is bestowed on the community so that it might recognise Christ's ministry in the ministry of the ordained.' (M M Schaefer and J F Henderson, *The Catholic Priesthood*, 88). This insight was never obscured in the Eastern church:

There is nothing given in the Church – be it ministry or sacraments or other forms of structure – which is not to be asked for as if it had not been given at all. This is the *epicletical* character of ecclesiology, evident in the first place in the eucharist itself which, although based on the given assurance of the words of institution, stands constantly in need of the invocation of the Spirit in order to be that which it is.

From John D Zizioulas, 'The Doctrine of God the Trinity Today: Suggestions for an Ecumenical Study,' in Alasdair I C Heron, ed, *The Forgotten Trinity. 3. a Selection of Papers Presented to the BCC Study Commission on Trinitarian Doctrine Today*, London, BCC/CCBI, 1991, pp 3-32, at p 28.

38. When the pastoral charge was replaced by a source of revenue as a 'title' to ordination, impetus was given to highlighting the ordination rite, thereby distancing it from the assembly. In turn this exaggerated the personal character and power to confect the eucharist. Chantry clerics ('massing priests') multiplied, who gained their living by offering stipendiary masses, mainly for the souls in purgatory. The teaching, guiding and caring

activities of the priesthood were sidelined. This contributed to the revival of the priesthood of the baptised under the Reformers. The call of the community for service was largely replaced by an individual's interior vocation. No longer was anyone compelled to be a bishop by a community, as were Augustine and so many others - as noted elsewhere by Eugene Duffy, 'Common Things Raised up to Angelhood.'

39. P E Fink ('The Sacrament of Orders,' 497) writes, 'The presider's book is the sacramentary, and the sacramentary is pre-eminently a book of prayer.' Cf J Thornhill, 'The Role of the Ordained Minister,' 201-202; Richard J Hauser, 'Priestly Spirituality,' *The New Dictionary of Sacramental Worship*, 1018-1024.

40. The Association of National Liturgy Secretaries of Europe, *Leading the Prayer of God's People: Liturgical Presiding for Priests and Laity*, Dublin, The Columba Press, 1991, p 11.

41. See J D Zizioulas, *Being as Communion*, 214-225, esp p 216.

42. David N Power OMI, writes:

When the words of consecration are accentuated as the moment of divine power, the minister stands alone, distinct from the body. When the communion is experienced as the moment of the Lord's presence and transforming power, then the people share in a mutual empowering in the Lord, and the minister's role is clearly a relationship to the body as such and one to be exercised in the midst of all. (In Michael A Cowan, ed, *Alternative Futures for Worship, Volume 6: Leadership Ministry in Community*, Collegeville, The Liturgical Press, 1987, p 91).

43. On possible improvements to the rite of prebyteral ordination, especially the light of a Church order of trinitarian communion ecclesiology, see also D N Power, *Leadership Ministry in Community*, 81-104, 142144; D L Gelpi, 'Priesthood,' *The New Dictionary of Sacramental Worship*, at pp 1017-1018, and Alan F Detscher, 'Ordination Rites', in the same work, pp 915-921, at p 920; M M Schaefer and J F Henderson, *The Catholic Priesthood*, 50; W J Rademacher, *Lay Ministry*, 100-102; G W Lathrop, 'Christian Leadership and Liturgical Community,' 120-121.

44. There would be practical difficulties arising from any admission of women to the presbyteral or episcopal colleges, eg, interpersonal, financial. But even so sober a scholar as Gustave Martelet SJ, discreetly warns about the hidden agendas still to be brought to the surface: 'Is one ever sure of being freed on this point [the interpretation of tradition as inalterable] from non-theological factors, and in this instance [the ordination of women], from socio-anthropological factors which even christianised humanity requires geological ages to leave behind?' (*Théologie du sacerdoce: Deux mille ans d'église en question. Tome III: Du schisme d'Occident à Vatican II*, Paris, Le Cerf, 1990, p 309, n 46).

45. From a vast literature note Prudence Allen, 'Integral sex, complementarity and the theology of communion,' *Communio* XVII (1990), 523-544; Gerald P Gleeson, 'The Ordination of Women and The Symbolism of Priesthood, Parts One and Two,' *The Australasian Catholic Record* lxvii (1990), 472-481; lxviii (1991), 80-88; Aidan Nichols OP, *Holy Order: The Apostolic Ministry from the New Testament to the Second Vatican Council*, The Oscott Series 5, Dublin, Veritas, 1990, pp 144-155, which includes, on pp 151-152, 'The apostolic ministry mediates the Son in his historical maleness; the Church community, typologically female, mediates the Spirit'; Hervé Legrand OP, '*Traditio perpetuo servata?* The Non-ordination of Women: Tradition or Simply an Historical Fact?' *Worship* 65 (1991), 482-508.

46. 'An ambassador represents the head of State. A British ambassador represents the Queen but he is not a representation of the Queen. He does not impersonate the Queen. He need not be a woman': Christopher Hill, 'The ordination of women in the context of Anglican/Roman Catholic dialogue,' *The Month* Vol CCLIII, No 1489 (January 1992), 6-13, at p 9 (following G W H Lampe). Calling a presbyter an 'icon' of Christ does not exclude women, since an icon is stylised and not lifelike. It might be more accurate to call the order of presbyterate the icon of Christ the Head, without descending to individual presbyters.

47. Peter E Fink SJ writes (in *A New Dictionary of Christian Theology*, article 'priesthood,' pp 464-466, at p 466):

Where in persona Christi is understood in a literal sense, the pressure is strong to retain an exclusively male priesthood. More than a question of mere practical decision, this issue urges the recovery of the priesthood of the corporate Church, and of the ministerial priesthood as representative embodiment of that corporate Church, where the Christ whose body is both male and female may find sacramental expression in both.

Compare in part Gisbert Greshake, *The Meaning of Christian Priesthood*, Dublin, Four Courts Press, 1988, p 88; M M Schaefer and J F Henderson, *The Catholic Priesthood*, 60-63, 88-89; M J Lawler, *A Theology of Ministry*, 91. 'It is only to the extent that they [believers] are ordained as representative vicars of the Church that they are ordained also as vicars of Christ, who is mysteriously one with the Church. Ordination establishes believers in an order of ministers who act directly in the name of the Church, and only indirectly in the name of Christ.'

48. See A Nichols, *Holy Order*, 156-157; Patrick J Dunn, *Priesthood: A Re-examination of the Roman Catholic Theology of the Presbyterate*, New York, Alba House, 1990, p 72.

49. Cf John Meyendorff, *Church History 2: Imperial Unity and Christian Divisions, The Church 450-680 A.D.*, New York, St Vladimir's Seminary Press, 1989, p 51. Some of the motivation for priestly celibacy is painfully conditioned by contemporary culture, eg, Stoic fear of genital pleasure, Neo-Platonic distaste for the body, and neo-levitical concern for ritual purity at the eucharist. Again, the emperor Justinian (527-565) prohibited the consecration of married men as bishops, lest their children inherit Church property. The Trullan Synod in Constantinople (AD 692) sanctioned this originally civil law (although its disciplinary decrees were rejected by the Pope). Probably concern to preserve the patrimony of the Church was a very minor contributing factor favouring the celibacy of the ordained in some regions.

50. The Decree on the Ministry and Life of Priests (actually, Presbyters), §16, is a fine statement of the value of presbyteral celibacy. There is no need to dwell on this here. See further, G Greshake, *The Meaning of Christian Priesthood*, 120-132; Jean Galot SJ, *Theology of the Priesthood*, San Francisco, Ignatius Press, 1985, pp 228-246; Joseph Cardinal Bernadin, 'Celibacy and Spirituality,' Origins Vol 20: No 19 (October 18, 1990), pp 300ff; John Paul II, *Pastores Dabo Vobis* in *Origins* Vol 21: No 45 (April 16, 1992), pp 717, 719-759, in §29 on pp 731-732. A Nichols (*Holy Order*, 164) aptly observes, 'To say that local Churches, in given parts of the globe, cannot be expected to produce celibate ministers of the Gospel is to say that they cannot be expected to reproduce an intrinsic element in the experience of the apostles. And this seems a strange way in which to recognise the Christian maturity of such churches!' See also R M Schwartz, *Servant Leaders of the People of God*, 27-28, 103-104, 120-123, 179-183.

51. J D Zizioulas, 'The Doctrine of God the Trinity Today,' 27-28.

'Common Things Raised up to Angelhood'
Priestly Formation Then and Now

Eugene Duffy

The First Vatican Council had only time to deal with the question of papal primacy. The Second Vatican Council tried to bring balance to the situation by considering the role of the bishops in the life of the Church. Somebody has said that another council will be needed to deal with a theology of the priesthood. In the meantime theorists and practitioners continue to debate the issue without arriving at any notable consensus. Much thought, too, has been given to the question of formation for priestly ministry, most recently in the Post-Synodal Exhortation of John Paul II, *Pastores Dabo Vobis* (March, 1992). If the Catechism of Trent described priests 'not merely as angels but gods,' recent documents are more earth-bound, at least easing the burden on formators. This essay looks at how priestly formation has developed over the centuries and, in the light of current needs, proposes some suggestions for formation in the future.

Formation in the early Church
We can hardly talk of priestly formation in the early Church because that ministry, as we know it today, cannot be readily identified with any one particular office in the Church. However, there was a variety of ministries, many of which have been absorbed into what is now recognised as priestly ministry. These included preaching, the celebration of the eucharist, leadership and administration. Because of the complexity of the question of priestly ministry and its precise development, and not least because of a lack of accurate historical evidence, it is almost impossible to talk of formation for any kind of ministry except in the most general terms.

The gospels, to a certain extent, provide us with some basic insights into the nature of formation in the early community. Jesus himself formed his disciples to continue his mission of preaching and manifesting the nature of the reign of God. The mission of the seventy-two reveals the core of what formation involved.[1] These disciples had obviously listened to Jesus teaching, observed him in the practice of his ministry – at prayer, sharing his table with the outcasts and destitute, healing the sick, consoling the bereaved and enjoying the delights of wedding feasts – they learned the trade from him as apprentices learn from the master. When they had acquired a certain familiarity and competence in the ministry he sent them out, two by two, to practise what they had learned. On their return there was a reflection on the exercise and further instruction on the nature of their mission, with an insistence that they keep the reign of God to the forefront of their minds and not become fascinated by their observable successes. They were given a basic but effective grounding in the ministry.

The other documents of the the New Testament do not give us any more information about the formation of those who exercise ministry in the community. However, the Pauline and other letters point to the high standards demanded of those who were to exercise ministry.[2] They were to be wholeheartedly devoted to Christ and his mission, imitators of him in the conduct of their lives and prepared to risk any hazards to make him known. The implication of the information we have must be that formation took place in the midst of the community and those who were considered suitable were nominated and appointed to fill various roles of public service in the Church. This is the situation which would appear to have prevailed for several centuries.

The patristic period
Throughout the patristic period, roughly the second to the fifth century, the situation with regard to formation remained relatively unchanged. There was obviously a growing clarification of ministerial roles in the Church, but this hardly impinged on the formation these ministers received. Jerome's protest at his choice for the presbyterate is indicative of the trend current in the late fourth century, that people were being chosen because of the outstanding witness

of their lives and not because they had been specifically trained or formed for office.

During this period the distinction between clergy and laity was not at all as clear or as well defined as it was soon to become. Lay people at this time took an active part in all aspects of the Church's life. They played an important part in the celebration of the liturgy, in the election of bishops and the nomination of presbyters; they helped to draw up an agenda for councils and participated in them; they administered Church property and preached. Jean Leclercq summed up the position thus:

> In brief we may say that laymen were recognised as being full-time Christians and were given full shares in Church affairs. There was no monopoly on the part of the clerics: they lived among the laymen, had the same way of life and manner of dress; they were urged to practise chastity, either within the married state or as celibates; they officiated at the altar and administered the sacrament of baptism. [3]

As regards recruitment the only condition required, according to Leclercq, was 'a certain standard of honest living.'[4] In conclusion we can say that formation was in exemplary living of the Christian life and not in any separate training programme either spiritual or intellectual.

Changes under Constantine

After the so called edict of Milan Christians enjoyed a new freedom in the empire. Christian ministers were favoured with the advantages and privileges of the pagan colleges of priests, were exempted from all duties of the empire and, in fact, as ministers of the cult gradually came to occupy a place of central importance in the empire. Schillebeeckx points out that at this time 'the ordinary believer was thus forced well into the background, and Christianity was narrowed down to a cultic community under the leadership of clerici ...'[5] The establishment of Christianity as the state religion by Theodosius in 380 added further to the problems created by the edict of Milan. While both emperors gave new freedom to the Church, their policies carried within them the seeds of trouble. As Christianity became more part of the imperial system, its ministers were more open to the danger of seeing themselves as public servants and functionaries, with the rights and privileges of civil administrators, subscribing to an ideology often far removed from the idealism of the gospel.

It is against this background of a developing clerical elite that the first signs of special formation for the clergy begin to appear. The earliest bishops who showed a concern for the formation of the diocesan clergy were St Eusebius (d.371) and St Paulinus (d.431). They combine a monastic discipline with a common life for the parochial clergy. However, the best documented of these efforts is that of St Augustine (d.430). He was particularly concerned about the formation of the clergy and the great care he took to ensure it led to a widespread reform of the Church in north Africa.

Before his own ordination, Augustine spent a few years enjoying the delights of what he called the *Christianae vitae otium*, a kind of cultured Christian retirement, where he and a small group of companions devoted themselves to contemplation and study, secluded from the cares of the world. The roots of this ideal existence were more in the tradition of pagan philosophers and retired administrators than in Christian monasticism. After his ordination, Augustine returned to Thagaste and with his companions, the *Servi Dei*, he combined this desire for contemplation with a vigorous defence of Christian doctrine in the face of threats posed by paganism, Donatism, and Manichaeism. Their combination of contemplation, study and pastoral action was remarkable, evidenced by the fact that so many of them were compelled to accept bishoprics in several dioceses of north Africa, including Augustine himself at Hippo.

When he went to Hippo, Augustine continued to gather a community around him and ensured the formation of the diocesan clergy. He did this at his own house near the principal church. This significance of this effort has been summarised variously by Augustine's biographers. Fredrick van der Meer said, 'The saint left behind him a seedbed of sanctity and what was really the first seminary for priests. It was an imperfect thing, but its essential features were to be repeated through the ages.'[6] And Peter Brown has shown that eventually these men formed by Augustine wielded more influence than many of the Roman governors, so much so that through their efforts 'all roads no longer led to Rome.' [7]

The Middle Ages

The seeds planted by Augustine bore fruit to the extent that there continued to be a concern for the formation of the clergy right up to our own time. This concern was realised with varying degrees of success over the centuries. At first it was taken care of by the monastic schools under the influence of Benedict and, more especially, Cassiodorus. These provided education for those aspiring to the monastic life in their conventual schools and for candidates for diocesan priesthood in their secular schools. These in turn were divided into major and minor schools. In the latter the fundamentals of Christian doctrine, chant, arithmetic and grammar were taught, and in the former theology and scripture. In many ways the arrangement was not unlike the later major and minor seminaries. [8]

Side by side with the monastic schools were the cathedral or episcopal schools. Pope Gregory the Great (d. 604) established such a school in Rome attached to the cathedral of St John Lateran and it has been described as the first pontifical seminary. At the Council of Toledo in 633 it was decreed that students destined for the priesthood should be trained in episcopal schools under the supervision of an experienced cleric of higher rank. These episcopal schools were generally staffed by the graduates of the monastic schools which were better equipped for their task.

Towards the end of the eighth century the formation of the clergy was given a fresh boost by the intervention of Charlemagne who decreed that all clerics must show an ability to read and write, as well as adequate competence in their professional duties, and this under the pain of suspension from office.

Much is made of the fact that the Church kept scholarship alive during the dark ages and that the clergy were among the few educated people in society. This needs to be tempered by two considerations. Firstly, the monastic and episcopal schools were so few in number that they were unable to provide even rudimentary training for many of the clergy, including those in urban settlements. As a result most clergy were educated by a kind of apprenticeship to the local pastor. In such circumstances the courses of instruction varied in content, duration and quality with the competence of the priest in charge. Secondly, it must be kept in mind that with the decline of Roman civilisation the place of civil officials was often taken over by the clergy who acquired a corresponding status in society, but one of privilege rather than competence. Thus one wonders about the motivation for educational accomplishment in such a context. Even the fact that theology was often used by ecclesiastics to bolster their claims for power over civil authorities[9] should put us on guard when evaluating their educational objectives.

The universities

The rise of the universities marked another phase in the formation of the clergy. The University of Paris grew out of the cathedral school of Notre Dame and other similar schools in the city. Shortly afterwards Oxford was established and in due course several others on the continent, including Rome, Padua, Bologna, Salamanca, Vienna and Prague. The impetus for learning was further accentuated in the early thirteenth century by the emergence of the mendicant orders. These new orders of Dominicans, Franciscans, Carmelites and Augustinians:

> swept all before them with their zeal, their eagerness for knowledge, and their systematic training for holy orders in the houses of study opened by their superiors in and around the universities. And for the masses, the friars' appeal was also enhanced by their poverty and by a kind of mystique concerning their way of life which created a vogue in European parochial circles that lasted beyond the mid-fourteenth century when they, too, began to undergo decline.[10]

Yet, despite this new enthusiasm for learning, a tiny minority of the clergy would have availed of a university education. This development had its negative effects. These new institutions were open to clergy and laity and very often discipline and morality were lax. Unless a student was in the house of a religious order there was little or no provision for his spiritual welfare. Most diocesan clergy were not provided for in this regard unless they were fortunate enough to be in residence with a pastor who cared for their spiritual well-being. Otherwise they were left to look after themselves. An even more serious problem for the majority was that the universities depleted the staffs of the cathedral schools of their best teachers and scholars. Consequently these schools declined and became little more than grammar schools or elementary theology schools.

The result of all these developments was that, as the middle ages drew to a close, the Church seemed to be pervaded by venality and hypocrisy and was ripe for dissolution. However, as Barbara Tuchman has said, 'An institution in command of the culture and so rooted in the structure of society does not easily dissolve.'[11] The problems which lay ahead were in no small way due to a clergy who were ill-disciplined, ill-educated and ill-formed for the responsibilities with which they were being entrusted. The situation was not to be remedied in any significant way until the Council of Trent.

The Council of Trent

Before Trent issued its canons on seminary formation, a number of significant efforts had already been made to reform the clergy and to provide them with suitable preparation for their ministry. Cardinal Ximenez, in Spain, founded a college at Alcala in 1500 with a faculty of forty-two professors. Although he set a headline which others followed, his efforts and those of his college of San Ildefonso were not enough to arrest the tide of decadence and dissipation which had overtaken the clergy. Just a week before he died, Luther was already posting his theses in Wittenberg. Even Adrian VI (d. 1523) admitted that many of the problems besetting the Church were the result of clerical malaise:

> We all, prelates and clergy, have gone astray from the right way, and for long there is none that has done good; no, not one ... each one of us must consider how he has fallen and be more ready to judge himself than to be judged by God in day of his wrath.[12]

Pope Paul III established a commission in 1536 to review the situation and to report back to him. The commission claimed that many of the scandals current and the decline in clerical standards could be traced to a laxity in admitting men to holy orders. They recommended vigilance in promoting candidates to the priesthood and suggested that each bishop should engage a teacher by whom minor clerics could be instructed in letters and morals. Interestingly, it did not occur to them to suggest establishing institutions specifically devoted to the formation of clergy.

The first real effort at providing a structured, formal education for the clergy was made by the Jesuits. They opened the Roman College in 1551, initially teaching the liberal arts, but from 1553 onwards teaching philosophy and theology. Three years later they opened the German College, again hoping to rescue the Church in Germany through well-trained pastors and preachers.

In England Reginald Pole, who was widely travelled in Europe and was a friend of St Ignatius, attempted a reform of the clergy through decrees passed at a national council in 1556. His main proposals were taken up at the Council of Trent in 1563 and in fact were incorporated into its legislation on seminaries with only slight amendments.

The Council of Trent decreed:

> that every cathedral, metropolitan and greater Church is obliged to provide for, to educate in religion and to train in ecclesiastical studies a set number of boys, according to its resources and the size of the diocese ... Those admitted ... should be at least twelve years of age, of legitimate birth, who know how to read and write competently, and whose character and disposition offer hope that they will serve in Church ministries throughout life.[13]

Students were to be taught in the humanities, 'the keeping of Church accounts and other useful skills' as well as 'scripture, Church writers, homilies of the saints, and the practice of the rites and ceremonies and administering the sacraments.'[14]

Although the decree called for a seminary in each diocese, it did not state that everyone to be ordained must be educated in a seminary. Furthermore, while its legislation on seminaries is regarded as one of the great achievements of Trent, it needs to be balanced by the consideration that the Council was more concerned with preventing the ordination of the unsuitable than providing for suitable training. Trent provided the broadest outlines for seminary formation but, in fact, its ideal was only slowly realised and amidst many difficulties.

The implementation of Trent

One of the first seminaries to be established pursuant of the new legislation was the Roman Seminary, later to be known as the Gregorianum. It was founded by Pius IV and entrusted to the care of the Jesuits. Others followed throughout Italy, most notably in the metropolitan district of Milan, under the energetic leadership of Charles Borromeo. He founded three seminaries in the city and three others within the northern province. He placed them under the direction of the Jesuits but soon had to withdraw them as many of the best students deserted the diocesan priesthood for the Society.

Elsewhere the implementation of the Tridentine decrees was uneven, reflecting historical circumstances and episcopal interest in priestly formation. The most important developments occurred in France in the seventeenth century. The giants of the reform were Adrien Bourdoise, Pierre de Berulle, Vincent de Paul, Jean-Jaques Olier and Jean-Marie Eudes. Berulle founded the French Oratory in 1611 with several companions. Their aim was the sanctification of diocesan priests and the restoration of their good reputation. Berulle was the key figure in this group because he imparted an understanding of priesthood and an accompanying spirituality which has remained until relatively recent times. He sought:

> the interiorisation of religion in the believer's identification through mental prayer with the attitudes and actions of Christ's life, regarded not simply as past events but as 'states' always available for contemplation. Priests and seminarians were to associate themselves with the role of the risen Christ as eternal

priest and victim. As priests they were representatives of Christ the victim-priest, imparting grace through the ministry of the sacraments. The seminarian's interior identification with Christ was accompanied by an attitude of self-abnegation, or even self-annihilation, so that Christ would live in him. [15]

Both Vincent de Paul and Jean-Jacques Olier were influenced by Berulle's spirituality and reforming enthusiasm. Vincent began his reform by initiating short retreats for those about to be ordained. These gradually became extended, paving the way for a more serious and thorough formation for seminarians. He was totally disillusioned by the efforts made in France and elsewhere at implementing the reforms of Trent and saw the need to separate the children who were coming forward for an ecclesiastical education from the young men who were anxious to present themselves for ministry.[16]

As Vincent was discovering the value of separating the children and the older candidates, Olier was following a similar plan in establishing the famous seminary of St Sulpice in the centre of Paris. From a parochial residence he sent his students to attend lectures at the Sorbonne and provided them with spiritual formation in their house of residence. This provided for a sound intellectual and spiritual formation of the candidates, as well as giving them a basic training in parish ministry, teaching catechism and assisting at the parish liturgies.

Gradually the Vincentians and Sulpicians were invited by the bishops of France to establish seminaries in their dioceses, a task accomplished during the eighteenth century. The effects of this achievement were widespread and long-lasting. They were sufficiently well established before the devastation of the revolution in 1789 to have provided a good foundation for the re-establishment which was to take place in the nineteenth century, not just in France but worldwide.[17]

Beyond the revolutions
The seminaries which emerged from the upheaval of the French revolution were in fact much more regimented than those which

they replaced. In the English-speaking world no seminaries had been established until after the revolution and so they developed their own features. Another revolution which had been taking place was the industrial revolution and it, too, had its bearing on the development of the seminary. Vincent J. Donovan has shown how the values inspired by the industrial revolution were transferred to the formation (production) of priests in the seminaries (priest factories).

Standardisation of the product and the means of production characterised industrial output. Now this applied to seminaries meant that a priestly mould was created and used universally. Seminarians studied the same textbooks in dogma, moral, canon law and liturgy through the medium of Latin. Their notion of what constituted holiness and what militated against it were standardised. Those who resisted this standardisation were removed as the faulty product was rejected on the assembly line.

Just as standardisation is necessary for large scale industrial production, so too is specialisation. In the seminaries specialists were employed in various areas of study to teach one particular subject. There was no mixing of dogma, moral, scripture, canon law or liturgy, and, perhaps even more devastating, prayer and spirituality were left to other experts in the interior domain. The idea of an integrated formation was lost sight of in a fascination with the success of specialisation. Both standardisation and specialisation were encouraged by the centralisation which was taking place in the Church under the leadership of Pius IX. The tendency to centralisation was a feature of the Church at the time because of the perceived threats from outside, but it was also one of the hallmarks of the industrial revolution.[18]

This survey of seminary formation in its broadest outlines may allow us to draw some worthwhile conclusions before considering the current state of the issue and the possibilities it may hold in store. The earliest, and possibly the best, formation for ministry took place in the midst of the community which was totally committed to the person of Christ and his mission. One was appointed to ministry by the community in virtue of one's outstanding fidelity to the gospel and so one could be relied upon to guide, lead and serve the community according to the mind of Christ. As the clergy became a more distinct group in the Church, and their formation became more separated from the formation of the entire people of God, there was always the risk that the standards of society and its evaluative criteria would influence formation more than zeal for the gospel and the spreading of the reign of God. This separate formation was at its best when the intellectual and spiritual formation were combined with an ardent desire to transform society in the light of the gospel. History also shows that a clergy well educated, not just in theology but in the liberal arts and philosophy, was indispensable in preserving the integrity of the Church whether threatened from within or without. Finally, a survey of developments up to Vatican II indicates that many of the features of the seminary are of relatively recent origin and that many of these have been enshrined in the law of the Church. Current needs of the candidates themselves and the needs of the Church may suggest that it is time many of these features were critically reviewed. The next section will look at some of these issues in the light of the most recent papal document on priestly formation.

The present situation
The standardisation and specialisation that characterised the seminaries which emerged after the French revolution have remained features of these institutions ever since. The *Decree on Priestly Formation* from the Second Vatican Council, and the Code of Canon Law promulgated in 1983, enshrine these qualities in their statements. The Code legislates for a six year programme, two years of philosophy and four years of theology, to be studied concurrently or consecutively. It requires residence in a seminary for the whole of this course and only in exceptional cases is this to be reduced to a minimum of four years.[19] It also states that different professors are appointed to teach each subject[20] and it envisages that 'students learn the whole of Catholic teaching.'[21]

While it has to be admitted that seminaries have served the Church extremely well in the past, this should not prevent us from asking questions about their continuation unchanged into the future. The fact that the Church's self-understanding has changed from being an institution to being a community of disciples[22] must be allowed to have an effect on the way its priests are formed and the kind of ministry they will be expected to perform.

There is also a lingering residue of Berulle's christology which encourages the segregation of future priests from the generality of the community of disciples. Here, too, the Church in its magisterial teaching has moved on. The ideal of Christ as the priest-victim is not that found in any current ecclesial documents. Rather they speak of Christ as head and shepherd.[23] This model of Christ for the priest suggests a more apostolic and collaborative style of ministry.

A renewed christology and ecclesiology tend to suggest that formation should be more carefully located in the community which the priest will eventually serve as leader and presider. While the laity are exhorted to pray for vocations to the priesthood, there is not yet sufficient encouragement for them to take a more active part in their formation. The RCIA programmes which have been well run in parishes may be a helpful model here. In the RCIA formation process not only is the candidate lead to a deeper conversion of life but the whole community is re-evangelised. If local communities were to be given more responsibility for forming their future ministers, is it not realistic to expect that the candidate and the community would both be brought to a deeper appreciation of the reign of God and of the place of ordained ministry in their midst?

A good grounding in the liberal arts, philosophy and the behavioural sciences could be taken at a third level college while the student had residence in a parish which would be attentive to his personal and spiritual well-being. Here he could participate actively in the liturgical life of the parish, be could receive spiritual direction and guidance from a competent director, be given considerable help in the area of personal and human development and participate in some of the pastoral programmes run by the parish. Such a process would facilitate a programme more sensitive to the individual needs of a candidate, be less pressurised than following a programme in a residential institution and afford the local community a role in the formation process.

Given the fact that today a growing number of lay people are more anxious to participate actively in the life of the Church, there is an increasing need for them, too, to be formed for their respective roles, especially in the areas of theology and spirituality. Currently the resources available for this formation are, for the most part, restricted to seminarians and religious. A more collaborative style of ministry could be fostered if both those preparing for the ordained and non-ordained ministry in the Church were being formed in closer association with one another. The need of the Church today for competent pastoral workers is enormous, thus pointing to the urgency for formation for a wide variety of ministers.

There are limited resources available to provide this formation. This leads to another important, if unsavoury, consideration with regard to seminary formation. At present the cost of taking a priest through a course of studies is extremely high and increasing in relation to the decline in numbers of seminarians.[24] In fact, these costs are so high that there is a reluctance to acknowledge them. If the seminary was seen as a resource centre for a local Church, then there would be more justification for financial investment in its resources.

A further question is thrown over the value of candidates for priestly ministry spending long periods in the one institution in the course of their formation. In fact their enthusiasm and idealism more often than not diminish rather than increase with the years. *Pastores Dabo Vobis* acknowledges this when it says, 'With priests who have just come out of the seminary, a certain sense of "having had enough" is quite understandable ...'[25] Indeed, the extended duration of the formation process often helps to create the illusion that at the end of it one knows enough, has acquired enough skill and virtue, to survive a lifetime of ministry and so become immune to the necessity for constant renewal and ongoing formation.

Pastores Dabo Vobis

Many of the foregoing observations may be countered in favour of continuing the present arrangement. However, they should not be readily passed over lest the seedbed go unweeded. The Pope's most recent statement on priestly formation gives weight to some of the issues raised above. It affirms the usefulness of the major seminary but it also suggests more flexibility with regard to formation than any previous document, for example:

> The *rationes* of the different nations or rites should be revised where opportune, whether on the occasion of requests made by episcopal conferences or in relation to apostolic visitations of the seminaries of different countries, in order to bring into them diverse forms of formation that have proved successful, as well as to respond to the needs of people with so-called indigenous cultures, the needs of the vocations of adult men, and the needs of vocations for the missions, etc. [26]

The document works on the assumption that those coming forward for formation will be those who have completed secondary education. However, the number of such students in the first world is decreasing and those referred to in the document as 'of adult age' are increasing. This calls for adaptation in the seminary and this is allowed for very explicitly:

> It is not always possible and often is not even convenient to invite adults to follow the educative itinerary of the Major Seminary ... what needs to be provided is some kind of specific programme to accompany them with formation in order to ensure, bearing in mind all the suitable adaptations, that such persons receive the spiritual and intellectual formation they require. [27]

The Pope also suggests that, prior to their admission to the major seminary, candidates should be given some basic formation so that they have a sufficiently broad knowledge of the faith. He encourages experimentation in this area and on the basis of the findings from this he has asked the Congregation for Catholic Education to communicate eventually with the episcopal conferences.[28] He is anxious too that those who come to the seminary via youth movements or associations should not have their links with them broken off, rather they should continue to be a source of encouragement and support.

In the context of ongoing formation for priests, the point is strongly made that the local community has a significant responsibility in this regard:

> Indeed the very relationship and sharing of life between the priest and the community, if it is wisely conducted and made use of, will be a fundamental contribution to permanent formation, which cannot be reduced to isolated episodes or initiatives, but covers the whole ministry of the priest. [29]

This principle could be applied to earlier stages of the formation process and may help to remind the future minister of his integral relationship with the community whom he serves.

These few excerpts from *Pastores Dabo Vobis* should not create the impression that the importance of the seminary has been played down. Nevertheless, they do alert those involved in the ministry of formation that they need to look carefully at the seedbed in which they are planting. In the words of Patrick Kavanagh, 'destiny will not fulfill unless you let the harrow play.' [30]

Conclusion

At a time when co-responsibility, collaboration and renewal are important considerations in the life of the Church, does it not make sense that priestly formation should take place in such a context? The Pope stresses and gives priority to human development in the formation of priests at every stage. Surely, if this is to he achieved it can only be in an environment and context which is a genuine reflection of the whole Church, lay, religious and ordained, young and old, male and female. Dialogue and serious exchange with all who are striving to live the Christian life to the full can only enrich and foster a spirit of dedication and commitment among those who are being called to a lifetime of service in leadership.

It may be that the time has come for the seminary to be an agent of formation for more than future priests. Maybe its role in the future is to facilitate the formation of a much wider group of people called to serve the Church in a variety of ministries. Within such a context future 'servant-leaders of the people of God' could be given a more intensive and shorter specialised formation for the exercise of their particular ministry. This could involve a time of residence towards the end of the formation period when the candidate, the community and those specifically charged by the Church with his care, could make that final discernment about his readiness for a permanent life committment to ordained minstry.

The seminary is never to be an end in itself, nor to be preserved for its own sake. It is there to serve the God who is calling people into a life of service and those who are doing their best to respond. To return to the simile from which the seminary gets its name: the gardener, believing in the power of the seeds to grow, prepares the soil, and does his best to ensure the right conditions for the growth of the plants; but he does not do the growing for it; it is the plant that grows.[31] Perhaps Paul said it better: I did the planting, Apollos did the watering, but God made things grow. Neither the planter nor the waterer matters: only God, who makes things grow. [32]

Notes

1   Lk 10:1-16.

2   Cf Acts 1:15-26; 1 Tim 5:17-25; Titus 1:5-9; 1 Pet 5:1-4.

3   'The Patristic and Medieval Church,' in *The Christian Priesthood*, eds Nicholas Lash and Joseph Rhymer, London, Darton, Longman & Todd; Denville, Dimension Books Inc., 1970, p 55.

4   *Ibid.*

5   *The Church with a Human Face: A New and Expanded Theology of Ministry*, translated by John Bowden, London, SCM Press, 1985, p 142.

6   Fredrik van der Meer, *Augustine the Bishop*, trs Brian Battershaw and G.R. Lamb, London, Sheed and Ward, 1961, p 234.

7   Peter Brown, *Augustine of Hippo*, London and Boston, Faber and Faber, 1967, p 145.

8   Yorke Allen, *A Seminary Survey*, New York, Harper & Brothers Publishers, 1960, p 348.

9   J. Leclercq, 'Patristic and Medieval Church,' p 15.

10 John Tracy Ellis, 'A Short History of Seminary Education I: The Apostolic Age to Trent,' in *Seminary Education in a Time of Change*, eds James M. Lee and Louis J. Putz, Tenbury Wells, Fowler Wright Books, 1965, p 11.

11 *A Distant Mirror: The Calamitous 14th Century*, New York, Ballantine Books, 1979, p 32.

12 Quoted by John Tracy Ellis, 'Seminary Education,' p 15.

13 Session XXIII, Decree on Reform, Canon 18 in *Decrees of the Ecumenical Councils*, Vol II, Ed Norman P. Tanner SJ, London, Sheed & Ward; Washington, Georgetown University Press, 1990, p 750.

14 *Ibid.*

15 Joseph M. White, 'How the Seminary Developed' in *Reason for the Hope: The Futures of Roman Catholic Theologates*, Wilmington, Michael Glazier Inc, 1989, p 12.

16 Pierre Coste, CM, *The Life and Works of St Vincent de Paul*, Vol. I, translated by Joseph Leonard, CM, London, Burns Oates & Washbourne, 1934, p 262-263.

17 When John Hand founded All Hallows College in 1842 he had already visited some of the Sulpician seminaries in France and decided to adopt their formation agenda for his new college. Cf Kevin Condon, *The Missionary College of All Hallows 1842-1891*, Dublin, All Hallows College, 1986, p 73.

18 *The Church in the Midst of Creation*, New York, Orbis Books, 1989, pp 35-47.

19 C.235.

20 C.253.

21 C.252.

22 This model of Church has been used by Pope John Paul in his first Encyclical *Redemptor Hominis* and most recently in *Pastores Dabo Vobis*. For a fuller treatment see Avery Dulles, *A Church to Believe In*, New York, Crossroad Publishing Company, 1985.

23 This image of Christ is the guiding one for the entire document *Pastores Dabo Vobis*.

24 In 1986-87 the average annual cost for a student in a seminary in the U.S. was $21,613(K. Schuth, *Roman Catholic Theologates*, p 77). Other expenses must be added to this, eg. book allowances, pocket money, travel allowances, medical care, etc.

25 Par 76; Research caried out by L.M. Rulla SJ, indicates that even after four years in houses of formation the change which has been effected in candidates is slight. Only about 2% are significantly helped to achieve greater personal maturity. Cf Roger Champoux SJ, in 'New Perspectives in Religious Formation,' reprinted from *Supplement to Doctrine and Life*, July/August,1977, p 216.

26 Par 61.

27 Par 64.

28 Par 62.

29 Par 78.

30 From 'To The Man After The Harrow', Patrick Kavanagh, *The Complete Poems*, Newbridge, The Goldsmith Press, 1972, p 10.

31 Cf Elizabeth Lawrence, *The Origins and Growth of Modern Education*, Harmondsworth, Penguin books, 1970, p 14f.

32 1 Cor 3:4-5.

Conclusion

All Hallows and the Irish Missionary Tradition
Re-Imaging the Myth

John Joe Spring

In my student days in All Hallows College, back in the early seventies, I can remember being intrigued by the late Fr Kevin Condon's frequent references to what he called 'the All Hallows myth and mystique.' Perhaps it sounded like too obscure a description of a reality that for us then was all too real and immediate. Or maybe the language of myth had not yet attained the level of theological respectability which it has today. Be that as it may, I have since become much more convinced of the appropriateness of Kevin's description. All Hallows was a particularly vibrant expression of the dramatic revival of interest in missionary evangelisation which occurred in the Irish Church around the middle of the last century. The emergence of such a strong missionary thrust against the grim social and economic climate of the time, and particularly its continued growth even during the disastrous famine years, does seem to demand an explanation beyond the purely historical or rational.

My own recently-acquired interest in exploring our Celtic roots convinces me that part of the explanation takes us back to the very origins of the Christian faith in these islands. Commentators on that period often express great surprise at how quickly the newly-planted Irish faith developed a strong missionary character. Long before the native Church could be said to have been built up internally historians speak of missionaries 'sweeping across Europe in waves.' Even after we have allowed ten per cent for Celtic exaggeration it is still an impressive picture!

It is hard to believe that within a century of the death of St Patrick (c. 463) one of his 'spiritual sons,' Colmcille, should be again heading across the Irish Sea to found the monastery of Iona, destined to become the centre providing the greatest impetus in the conversion of England. Not many years later (c. 590) Columbanus and his twelve companions were setting out from Bangor, faced with the daunting task of bringing the light of the gospel to a Europe still reeling from the break-up of the Roman Empire and the ravages of the 'barbarian invasions.' In all, he and his monks would found over a hundred monasteries, some of them to become the greatest strongholds of faith and learning in the middle ages.

These are perhaps the best known of the great wave of *peregrini pro Christo* from the first great missionary period of the Irish Church – the sixth to the ninth century. But they were certainly not an isolated few. The litany could continue with hundreds of other names, such as Aidan, Gall, Kilian, Fursey – besides the thousands whose names are known only to God. What was it that inspired so many of our ancestors to undergo that 'white martyrdom' of exile and isolation as witnesses to the new-found faith? How did the gospel mandate to 'Go, make disciples of all nations ...' find such an immediate and fruitful response?

I suspect that the explanation for these questions has more than a purely historical relevance for us today. At a time when the Church at home and abroad is being challenged to respond to the urgent need for 'a new evangelisation,' I feel that such an exploration can put us in touch with what is deepest and most distinctive within our own missionary tradition.

But before we journey back too far into the Celtic mists, I would like to look a little more closely at this 'All Hallows myth' which so absorbed Kevin Condon and which is a more accessible expression of our missionary tradition. As All Hallows celebrates its 150th Anniversary, I suppose it is inevitable that it pays some attention to reviewing the statistics. By any standards they are remarkable. Since its foundation in 1842 approximately four thousand priests have been ordained from the College for service in all corners of the English-speaking world and beyond. From an Ireland still reeling from the devastation of the famine, students were volunteering in rapidly-increasing numbers for mission, especially to the so-called 'new territories.' For some it meant the daunting journey to the high veldt of South Africa, for others the remote parts of the yet to be unionised States of America, for others the Australian outback, while a smaller number became involved in the missions to India and Argentina. Nearer home many more were responding to the challenging call for priests to serve the very urgent needs of the post-Famine Irish diaspora in the over-crowded cities of England and Scotland. The following chart, compiled by Kevin Condon for the *All Hallows Annual* of 1953,[1] represents a remarkable story of courage and commitment during the first four decades of the College's existence.

	1845-1865	1866-1880	Total
Australia and New Zealand	80	170	250
Canada	25	35	60
Great Britain	130	60	190
India	25	5	30
South Africa	17	11	28
United States of America	200	220	420
West Indies, Argentine	36	13	49
Miscellaneous	13	16	29
Total	526	530	1,056

What the statistics – impressive though they are in themselves – can never give us, of course, are the varied personal stories of the individual missionaries and of the families and communities they left hehind. Kevin Condon's history[2] of the first fifty years of the College gives us brief glimpses of some of the personal stories involved but he would have been the first to admit that such details are painfully limited. We can only speculate about what was in the mind and heart of the young William Gleeson as he boarded a sailing ship for India in 1854; or of Andrew Twomey heading for the 'wild west' of America, having to travel as far again by river boat and horse-back when the ocean crossing was completed; or of William McGinty, the first of the large contingent who would embark on the four month sail to Sydney. And what were the thoughts and feelings of the parents and brothers and sisters as they received what must have been understood then as a final blessing from a beloved son or brother embarking on such voyages? Again we can only imagine, but we may safely assume that every human emotion was evoked from profound agony to high ecstasy.

The missions to which many of these early pioneering priests went must have been extremely demanding – physically, emotionally and otherwise. For example, when the already-mentioned William McGinty eventually arrived in the vast diocese of Sydney in 1846, he was given responsibility for an area of over three thousand square miles, which included a widely scattered community of 900 Catholics. It is hard for us to imagine the hardship of such a mission in the primitive state of travel pertaining there at that time. His nearest priest colleague was forty-five miles away. Such examples could be multiplied. Not surprisingly, many succumbed to the harsh conditions, suffering illness and early death.

A particularly tragic casualty was Joseph Rooney in Agra, India, who together with a large number of innocent civilians was killed in what came to be known as the Cawnpore massacre. But far from being daunted by these reports,slowly filtering back to the College, the next generation of young hopefuls seemed to have been inspired by them, offering themselves in increasing numbers as the statistics clearly show.

Perhaps it is also well to keep in mind at this point that All Hallows was only one, albeit a numerically significant one, of several Irish missionary colleges and institutes, both male and female, which were operating at this time.[3] St Kieran's, Kilkenny, St Patrick's, Carlow, Maynooth College, St John's, Waterford, St Peter's, Wexford, although founded as diocesan or national seminaries, were all responding in various degrees to the overseas mission, particularly the needs of the widely-scattered emigrant Irish diaspora. And from around the same time as the founding of All Hallows, several religious orders of women were responding with courage and commitment to the call of the wider apostolate. Even prior to this, many Irish girls had been recruited by French missionary orders for work on the foreign missions. One other missionary initiative worthy of note in this context is that of the Vincentian mission to China. While in its early stages this involved only small numbers of Irish priests, supplementing their French confreres, it seems to have made a deep impact, probably because of the extraordinary level of heroism it demanded.

The foregoing examples are enough to indicate that the All Hallows mission, founded by John Hand, was not an isolated phenomenon, though it did have unique features. It can more properly be seen as a distinctive but integral part of the re-awakening of that missionary tradition which had for too long been stifled by a combination of socio-economic oppression and draconian penal laws. The way in which the tradition was revived again, as soon as emancipation had been achieved (1829) and despite the other negative factors already noted, is perhaps the best proof of its durability and vitality. Indeed, it seems most appropriate that the great architect of Catholic emancipation himself, Daniel O'Connell, should also have played a significant part in the origins of All Hallows. It was from him as Lord Mayor of Dublin that John Hand acquired the lease of Drumcondra House, soon to become All Hallows Missionary College.

When we consider the tremendous amount of zeal and commitment represented in all those various missionary endeavours, we do not need to make any apology for seeing those involved as worthy heirs of the earlier generations of monastic missionaries. Indeed,they had many characteristics in common: a deep personal love for God's Word; a passionate commitment to sharing it with others; and a strong spirit of self-sacrifice. As we asked about the first missionaries, so we may well ask about their successors: What was it that inspired and sustained them?

Such a question,of course, must ultimately confront us with mystery – the mystery which is at the heart of all God-given vocation. But on the principle that grace builds on nature, we can legitimately ask whether there is something at the level of the human psyche which has enabled successive generations of Irish missionaries to interpret and respond to that vocation as consistently as they have

done. My own view is that there is such a 'nurturing myth' underlying it all – a variation on the universal hero myth which was particularly popular in Celtic mythology and legend. Many of us will
be familar with the basic pattern from childhood stories of the Fian-
na, Oisín, Fionn MacCumhail,Eachtra Airt Mhic Choinn and many
others. Typically the hero is called to undertake some great quest or
adventure on behalf of his people; it will usually involve leaving
the clan and undertaking a difficult journey; he receives some help
and advice to prepare him for the ordeals ahead; he will encounter
many difficulties, natural and super-natural; finally he achieves the
object of his quest and returns to his people, he and they both enriched by the experience. In some of the tellings, however, this final
stage involves the ultimate sacrifice for the hero.

One doesn't have to use too much imagination to see how this Celtic hero provided an inspiring role-model for the first Christian
missionaries. Many of the more dramatic versions of the early lives
of the saints have to be seen in this light. The Celt was not too scru-
pulous about letting the facts get in the way of a good story! The
new Christian role-models had to be seen to be at least as brave and
as virtuous as were their pagan counterparts. Even the life of Christ
could be presented in terms of the ultimate hero's journey, under-
taken on behalf of the whole human family. The parallels are easy
to see.

To come back to the All Hallows story, it seems to me that this too
is a good example of the enduring quality of the nurturing myth. In
the Maynooth of the eighteen thirties when John Hand, this frail
farmer's son from Oldcastle, began to share his vision of founding a
missionary college, it must have sounded very much like the impossible dream. He had plenty of advisers to tell him that the circumstances or the times were not right. When, eventually, he got to
the stage of formally presenting his project to the Irish Bishops, the
response was not very encouraging to say the least. Most of them
had, we are told:

> the strange notion that the balance of Fr Hand's reason was dis-
> turbed … and that his judgement could not be trusted in the
> affair.[4]

Fortunately, perserverance is one of the outstanding qualities of the hero in all the best stories. Obviously, it was a quality not lacking in John Hand. He pleaded, persuaded, and bullied, as the occasion seemed to warrant, until the dream at last became reality on 1 November 1842. The low-key account of the inauguration held little promise of future achievement. According to a memoir of his first associate, Bartholomew Woodlock:

> About the middle of October Mr Hand placed the first student in the College ... On the Solemnity of All Saints 1842, the titular feast of the College, there were three Masses in the house which for want of better accommodation, were celebrated on a small cabinet or side-board, in the drawing room and in borrowed vestments.[5]

The Mass which was celebrated to launch the one hundred and fiftieth jubilee celebrations on 1 November 1991 was less restrained. Archbishop Desmond Connell of Dublin presided over a packed Church in giving thanks for the four thousand priests from the College who, over the years, have responded to the gospel mandate expressed in its motto, Euntes, docete omnes gentes. The gathering also included representatives of the thousands of alumni who studied there for various periods but decided to pursue other vocations in life.

But there was a significant new constituency also well represented at this celebration. It was that of the growing number of religious and lay men and women who now pursue a variety of courses for mission and ministry side by side with the seminarians. As the number of seminarians in All Hallows has declined, in common with most other missionary institutes, it is interesting to note the destinations of the recent graduates of one of its newer pastoral courses: Argentina, Brazil, South Africa, Australia, New Zealand, Tunisia, Malta, Zambia, Korea, Canada, Florida, Venezuela, France, Britain and Ireland, north and south, – and that from a class of forty-eight. The nurturing myth may have to be re-interpreted in response to changing circumstances; its power to inspire would seem to remain as strong as ever.

Notes

1   *All Hallows Annual*, 1953-54, p 171.

2   Kevin Condon, *The Missionary College of All Hallows 1842-91*, Dublin, All Hallows, 1986, pp 93-122.

3   See Edmund M. Hogan, *The Irish Missionary Movement*, Dublin, Gill and Macmillan, 1990.

4   Condon, *All Hallows*, p 18.

5   Woodlock MS, quoted in Condon, *All Hallows*, p 60.

The Contributors

REV PATRICK COLLINS CM lectures in spirituality at All Hallows College. He is the author of *Intimacy and the Hungers of the Heart* (1991).

REV DR EAMONN CONWAY is a lecturer in systematic theology at All Hallows College.

SISTER MOYA CURRAN OP is a psychotherapist and head of the Pastoral Department at All Hallows College.

REV DR THOMAS CURRAN from the diocese of Palmerstown North, New Zealand, is working with the Irish Columbans in Peru.

REV EUGENE DUFFY is a lecturer in systematic theology at All Hallows College.

TESS HARPER lives on Inishmore in the Aran Islands where she is a member of a lay community.

REV DR THOMAS LANE CM is a former president of All Hallows College.

REV DR JAMES H. MURPHY CM is a lecturer in literature at All Hallows College.

REV DR BRIAN M. NOLAN CM is a lecturer in Sacred Scripture and systematic theology at All Hallows College.

REV THOMAS MCHUGH is the director of the Christian Education Centre in the Archdiocese of Southwark.

REV JOHN JOE SPRING directs the lay ministry programme at All Hallows College. He was formerly head of the Catholic Missionary Society in London.

REV ROBERT WHITESIDE lectures in pastoral care and directs the pastoral formation programme at All Hallows College.

Related titles from The Columba Press

What are We At?
Ministry & Priesthood for the Third Millennium

Michael Casey

What are the struggles of being a priest today? Why is there a crisis? Why is there confusion about the role of the priest? Why does the Church seem to be losing contact with the lives of the plain people?

Do our Church thinking and structures come in the way of the gospel today? Must we make a new beginning, as John Paul II said in Knock in 1979?

Here is one priest's story of his struggles with the credibility gap between 'the Church' and the real world of today and his suggestions for rethinking and reforming ministry and priesthood at the beginning of the Third Millennium.

Fr Michael Casey has been a priest for twenty-five years and has served in parishes both comfortable and deprived. Recently he took time off to go away to study and reflect on his experiences, hoping to suggest ways and means of adaptation in the Church so that it might more adequately respond to the needs of the people of the modern world.

ISBN 1 85607 049 2

Price £9.99

Related titles from The Columba Press

Intimacy
and the Hungers of the Heart

Pat Collins CM

Intimacy and the Hungers of the Heart maintains that we can be no closer to God than we are to our true selves, to other people, and to the created world about us. Using the best insights of modern psychology, science and spirituality, it explores how contemporary Christians can move from alienation to a sense of intimate connection with the whole of created reality. Part one shows how to be intimate with oneself by means of growing self-awareness. Part two describes how one can be intimate with nature and other people by means of honest self-disclosure and loving attention. Part three shows how the firs two forms of intimacy can lead to an intimate relationship with the Mysterious Other who is 'published and made known' as the Beyond in the midst of our everyday lives.

Fr Pat Collins CM is an Irish Vincentian priest. He is a lecturer in Spirituality at All Hallows College, Dublin, and at the International Institute of St Anselm in England. In 1987 his *Vi Daro Un Cuore Nuovo* was published in Italy and his most recent book is *Maturing in the Spirit*, which was commissioned by the Charismatic Renewal in Ireland

ISBN 1 85607 0271

Price £8.99